LOOKING *at* TOURISM

DERRICK ANDERTON

Hodder & Stoughton

A MEMBER OF THE HODDER HEADLINE GROUP

British Library Cataloguing in Publication Data

Anderton, Derrick
  Looking at Tourism
  I. Title
  338.4791

ISBN 0 340 59811 5

First published 1995
Impression number   10 9 8 7 6 5 4 3 2 1
Year   1999 1998 1997 1996 1995

Typeset by Wearset, Boldon, Tyne and Wear.
Printed in Great Britain for Hodder & Stoughton Educational, a division of Hodder
Headline Plc, 338 Euston Road, London NW1 3BH by Page Bros, Norwich.

Contents

1 Who are the tourists and why do they tour?

Tourism is not a them and us situation. The questions posed in the chapter title affect all of us. There are no longer two distinct classes of people, one mobile and one static: we are all tourists to some degree or another. In the world of today, few of us stay put all the time and most of us have had the experience of being visitors in other people's villages, towns, cities and regions. Many of us have, in addition, travelled to countries abroad to admire the landscapes, customs and historical monuments that we believe to be either our European or our world heritage. Other people, in turn, come as tourists to the areas where we live; sometimes we are visitors and sometimes we are hosts.

There is nothing new in this – a floating population of explorers, pilgrims and traders has been moving about the Earth since earliest times – what is new is the rapidly increasing speed of travel and the growing volume of travellers. For instance, according to a forecast from the 1993 Aerotech Exhibition at the NEC Birmingham, the average annual growth of airline passenger travel is about 6 per cent per year, and more than 8,000 new aircraft will be delivered over the next 15 years (see Chapter 5 for a fuller examination of this issue). Clichés like 'the global village' and 'our shrinking planet' are true now as never before.

This book will attempt to examine the size and nature of increasing visitor demand and its impact upon destinations and populations. The most undesirable effects of tourism are those which threaten the surface of the Earth, as well as the seas and the atmosphere which surround it. Attention will be paid, therefore, to the prospects for sustainable and 'green' tourism. It will also be necessary to look at how tourism operates and how it is organised and managed, in order to discover positive ways in which it can continue to function for everybody's good.

All change tends to disorientate and frighten. The increasing number of tourists sometimes makes us feel that we are being invaded. We feel insecure because long-established barriers are coming down and unfamiliar faces crowd around us; we complain that more always means worse. Ordinary individuals, living every-day working lives, can easily be overwhelmed by the effects of the rise and rise of tourism.

Looking on the positive and practical side of things, however, it soon becomes clear that the tourism industry contributes substantially to people's wealth and welfare, as well as to their enjoyment and enlightenment. At its best, tourism can broaden minds, give pleasure and widen horizons without harming the Earth or disappointing our own or other people's expectations. Travel is still the greatest power for spreading the knowledge and understanding that are vital to preserve the world in which we live.

The scale of the industry

Currently, international tourism is considered by some to be the most important industry in the world. In November 1991 *Tourism* (the journal of the Tourism Society) quoted a statement by the World Travel and Tourism Council (WTTC) which stated: 'Travel and tourism is the world's largest industry and the major contributor to economic development.' Other authorities only put tourism in second place, but all the experts forecast that it will continue to grow, and to such an extent that by the year 2000 it will certainly be ahead of all the others.

There is no doubt that tourism is Britain's biggest overseas earner. The following 1991 figures from the British Tourist Authority (BTA) prove that it is well ahead of other industries:

Table I Earnings of tourism compared with other UK leading exports (1991)

	£(billions)
All services	32
Tourism	7.5
Petroleum products	6.8
UK financial institutions	4.5
Civil aviation	3.9
Sea transport	3.7
Textile	2.3

It is strange perhaps to think of holidays and travel as creating more employment and wealth than, say, the oil or textile industries, but it must be remembered that a lot of what is classified as tourism consists of journeys undertaken for the purposes of business and education.

The sums generated by the travel industry world-wide are quite staggering. In 1990, for example, approximately 425 billion international travellers spent more than £128 billion around the globe. One in every 15 employees – 112 million people world-wide – is involved in this sector.

Business advantages for Britain

In this growth market the UK tourism industry takes fifth position in the world tourist league; only the USA, Spain, France and Italy earn more. The UK figures speak for themselves:

- tourism represents 3 per cent of total national output (Gross Domestic Product (GDP))
- the industry contributes over £22 billion to the British economy each year (this figure includes all earnings from internal tourism)
- invisible overseas earnings from tourism are £7.5 billion
- the Treasury gains £2.3 billion in VAT each year
- 1.5 million people are directly and indirectly employed in the industry
- tourism helps to support the arts, entertainment and catering industries, and other leisure facilities and services
- tourism encourages investment in the environment and heritage, thus helping to create and maintain attractive places in which to live and work.

(Source: 'Big Business for Britain',
Tourism Society Report, 1990.)

In addition, about 50,000 large and small private- and public-sector British businesses are directly involved in tourism. Some examples are:

- hotels and guest houses; self-catering accommodation (holiday flats, villas, cottages, time-share apartments, Scandinavian lodges, chalets, canal and river boats)
- holiday centres, worlds and parks, caravan parks, holiday villages, camping sites
- sun centres, waterworlds, sun parks, theme parks, amusement parks, heritage attractions, post-industrial nostalgia attractions, wildlife parks, ski centres, working farms
- tour operators, travel agents and other travel organisers.

Even more businesses and services (upwards of 150,000) are indirectly involved in tourism, for instance:

- restaurants, cafés, pubs, clubs, other food and beverage (F & B) outlets
- airports, sea ports, hovercraft termini, ferry operators, rail termini, Channel Tunnel, bus companies, motorway and road networks
- leisure centres and sports centres, arenas and stadiums
- golf courses and sailing marinas
- theatres, cinemas, concert halls
- museums and galleries.

Another feature which makes tourist support for business encouraging is the steady yearly increase in the numbers of holidaymakers. Tourism is an industry which, as Table 2 clearly shows, has not yet reached its peak. Particularly interesting is the increase in sums spent on holidays abroad. This is still good business for Britain, since, apart from the increased turnover at airports, sea ports and so on, most holidays abroad are paid for in Britain before departure. Such increases in spending are good news for UK travel agents and tour operators, who are the major direct employers of the industry.

Table 2   Estimated expenditure[1] on holidays taken by the British[2]

Year bp	Britain £ million	Abroad £ million	Total £ million
1978	1,700	1,860	3,560
1979	2,380	2,570	4,950
1980	2,420	3,510	5,930
1981	2,710	4,320	7,030
1982	2,500	4,730	7,230
1983	2,640	5,000	7,640
1984	2,970	5,560	8,530
1985	3,080	6,140	9,220
1986	3,050	6,740	9,790
1987	3,100	8,500	11,600
1988	3,740	9,140	12,880
1989	3,820	10,150	13,970
1990	4,140	10,640	14,780

[1]All expenditure is included, i.e. accommodation, travel to and from destination, and incidental expenditure. The figures include expenditure on behalf of accompanied children in adult-holiday expenditure parties.
[2]Adults and children accompanying them.
Source: *British National Travel Survey*, the British Tourist Authority's annual survey.

Future prospects

Prospects for the future can never be accurately predicted, because of the changing tastes of tourists and also because of new measures which governments bring in from time to time. In its report *Guidelines for Tourism to Britain 1993–97*, the BTA expresses various concerns about Government action (or lack of it). For instance, it is worried that the service provided by the Channel Tunnel could result in a net loss to British tourism, because Britons, being able to get abroad more easily, will spend money in Europe rather than in the home market. Furthermore, the BTA asks whether the Government could do more to make Britain more attractive to incoming visitors using the tunnel. Effective measures could include:

- a revision of Sunday trading laws to bring the UK more in line with the rest of the world
- further reform of licensing hours
- directives to F & B outlets which would result in easier availability of food and drink, fixed-price menus and a more welcoming attitude towards children
- implementing plans for the high-speed rail link from Dover to London without delay
- modifying plans for rail privatisation and motorway charges which might deter incoming tourists
- insisting that the distinctive red livery of London's buses is maintained after the deregulation of London Transport.

The BTA estimates that if the Government worked in harmony with the industry, the 18.5 million overseas visitors who came to Britain in 1993 could be increased to 24 million by 1997.

Some terms used in the industry

Travel is a necessary part of tourism; but is tourism a necessary part of travel? Providers of tourism services have tried to answer this question by considering the point of departure, the means of transport used, the destination, the purpose of travel and how long it takes. They have come up with some straightforward and simple answers:

- *domestic tourism* is tourism within one's own country
- *foreign tourism* takes one outside one's own country
- *outgoing tourism* means all tourist traffic leaving a country
- *incoming tourism* refers to all traffic entering a country
- *touring* means visiting several places on one holiday, rather than aiming for a single destination. This form of

tourism expanded greatly with the coming of motor coaches and the mass production of cars and is still popular today.

- *Tourism* itself is difficult to pin down exactly, because of the great variety of reasons why people travel, but the Tourism Society of Britain, founded in 1977, provided an excellent definition: 'The temporary, short-term movement of people to destinations outside the places where they normally live and work and their activities during the stay at these destinations.' This definition (from the Government's Task Force report *Tourism and the Environment*, 1992) covers visits for most purposes including business, conferences, conventions, travel for study purposes, and visits to friends and relatives (VFR). It also includes day visits from home for leisure and recreational purposes.
- *Tourists* are defined by the World Tourist Organisation (WTO) as: 'All visitors making at least one overnight stay; a temporary visitor, staying in a country for at least 24 hours for one of the following range of reasons: leisure (i.e. recreation, holiday, health, study, religion, sport); business; family; conference or mission.'
- An *international tourist trip* is defined by the European Travel Monitor (an annual digest of tourism facts and figures) as: 'One lasting one night or more, for any purpose, outside the country of origin.'

This is all summed up by an international agreement which was formulated as far back as 1963:

> The tourist industry is held to encompass travel for business, education, religion, visits to friends and relatives, health, sport and fitness activities as well as holidays.

The essential point about tourism, whether for recreation or business purposes, is that it is a circular journey. It may go to various places and it may occupy differing periods of time, but it always ends up back at the starting point.

Tourism always implies at least a one-night stay away from home, otherwise the journey would be regarded as a *trip* or *excursion*. The question then arises: how long in both time and distance is a trip? For the purpose of statistical assessment the English Tourist Board (ETB) regards a leisure trip as being at least a 20-mile round journey, or one having a duration of at least three hours.

The term *weekend break* seems to be pretty well self-explanatory, but there is a distinction to be made with the *long weekend break* which runs from Friday to Monday. The ETB regards a holiday lasting three days or more, but less than a week, as a *short break*. In addition the BTA, the compilers of the *British National Travel Survey* (BNTS), regard four nights and upwards as a *long holiday*. This minimum of four nights hardly seems to justify the description 'long', but is meant to make a distinction between a main holiday and a short break.

Changing attitudes of both visitors and businesses

Over the years the words 'tourist', 'tripper' and 'excursionist', though accurate, have gathered overtones of disapproval and ridicule. In the early years of mass tourism the phrase 'package tourist' diminished the status of travellers to other countries. Holiday companies and the resorts, therefore, now like to refer to their clients as *visitors*. In today's world this does sounds better, and such small touches indicate a more sophisticated tourist industry. 'Visitor' conjures up the idea of old-fashioned hospitality, of guests and hosts. There are implications of a personal, social and cultural exchange, though, of course, everyone knows that money is involved. Also, perhaps, if clients are regarded and treated as responsible guests, their own attitudes may be more consistently sensible and considerate.

The benefits of a good image

The ETB is trying to encourage tourism businesses to give a better service to visitors and an improved image to the industry. In 1991, for example, they unveiled a new code of practice for tourist attractions by the terms of which operators must ensure:

- adequate parking, catering and toilet facilities
- clearly stated entry charges and details of any additional charges once inside
- high standards of cleanliness, courtesy and maintenance
- access for disabled visitors.

Operators observing the code will be able to display the ETB logo and promotional material on their premises, and will be promoted by the ETB and regional tourist boards. The point of the new code is also to set standards. With sightseeing in the UK reaching a record figure of 349 million visits in 1991, which generated £800 million in revenue (ETB figures), the scheme makes good business sense as well as preserving national and professional pride.

The Welsh Tourist Board (WTB) is making a determined effort to attract people to its area. The following story from the *Daily Mail* describes a worthwhile initiative which should make life in Wales more pleasant for everyone.

Charming wardens

Traffic wardens are being sent to 'charm school' in a bid to cheer up tourists. Welsh wardens are to attend one-day seminars stressing the importance of 'interpersonal, communication, and customer service skills.'

The Welcome Host Scheme is aimed at protecting Wales's £1.4 billion-a-year tourism industry by encouraging workers who deal with the public – railway porters, cab drivers, shop assistants and bus drivers – to be charming and courteous.

This policy of giving a high profile to civility and service does seem be successful. Senior economists are predicting that Wales will emerge as one of the most prosperous regions in the European Union. A continuing campaign – 'Escape to our beautiful landscapes' – has boosted tourism in Wales by raising public awareness of the principality as a high-quality tourist destination, and up to 20 per cent of employed people are now working in tourism in rural Wales.

Garden Festival Wales, the last of five major British festivals, attracted nearly 3 million visitors in 1992. Its aim was to change visitors' perception of a former industrial blackspot in Ebbw Vale, and to show that the valleys of South Wales are getting greener. The WTB has stated that the short-break and day-visitor market has expanded rapidly since the festival. The WTB estimated that in 1993 the day-visitor market for the whole of Wales reached 32 million – and this figure is likely to grow each year. The short-term economic and environmental aim of this regeneration in Ebbw Vale was to beautify the valley, increase the tourist trade and raise European awareness of the area. The longer-term benefit is that permanent residential property and facilities for light industry will be built as part of a £1 billion Government development, which has also attracted EU aid. This means much-needed jobs in a region which has lost its extractive industries.

Unwelcome visitors

The above is a good example of the hosts trying to be more hospitable, friendly and accommodating. There are still, however, too many visitors who make themselves unwelcome by causing stress to others and serious trouble for themselves simply because of ignorant or thoughtless behaviour. These people are perhaps best thought of as 'holiday takers' rather than holidaymakers – they certainly do not make a holiday for those around them, especially if they eat and drink themselves sick and silly! In some places the hosts have decided that enough is enough. Dick Welch, vice-president of the Balearic Travel Association, writes in the *Mail on Sunday*, July 1993:

> This week 25,000 British tourists have arrived on Majorca, the island I love. They will enjoy our beaches, cafés, hotels and sunshine, for Majorca is still the most popular foreign holiday destination for the British. But by this time next year there will not be so many British coming to Majorca. We have decided that we no longer wish our island to be the paradise for the lager lout, the young single man who only wants to come here to drink himself into oblivion, then cause trouble on our streets, and sleep it all off on our beautiful shores ... now we have decided to change. Many of the cheap hotels are being converted into flats for the Majorcis themselves. We are deliberately reducing our tourist beds by 80,000 ... Not all the English-style pubs and cafés will disappear, but they will be encouraged to cater for families rather than just pump out lager. And the truth is that the British lager lout, whose main desire is to create merry hell on a Saturday night, will no longer be welcome.

In case we should take too gloomy a view of the Majorcan situation we should note that Señor Jaime Cladera, minister for tourism for the Balearic Islands (which include Majorca), received in 1991 the first 'World Aware' award. When presenting this new prize for environmental improvement, the managing director of Thomson Holidays said: 'In less than two years the transformation of the Islands inspired by Señor Cladera has set an example which other countries would do well to follow.' The findings of research by Lunn Poly confirmed that British holidaymakers were returning to Majorca once again. The company said that three out of every five holiday bookings it had taken for 1994 were to Spanish destinations. Majorca alone accounted for 20 per cent of the total. The message is clear: a clampdown on bad behaviour allied with environmental reform can restore the reputation of a run-down resort.

Tourism associated with sport can also give rise to scandalous behaviour by so-called fans, as related by the *Shopshire Star* in the following reports. The first refers to one of the rounds for the 1992 European Cup:

ENGLISH FANS ON RAMPAGE

About 200 drunken English soccer fans smashed shop windows, damaged cars and brawled with Germans in Berlin last night.

Six were detained and later released after they had sobered up. They had stopped over in Germany on the way to Poland for England's game.

And in 1993 the situation had got no better . . .

ANOTHER 195 FANS ADD TO SHAME

Another 195 British soccer hooligans were arrested in Amsterdam's second night of violence – bringing the catalogue of shame in the build-up to tonight's World Cup clash to almost record proportions.

And again in 1993 . . .

BOOTING OUT THE BIG MATCH THUGS

More than 70 England soccer fans were expected to be deported from Norway today after rioting which caused damage estimated at more than £100,000. The trouble started after midnight when the fans wrecked the Paleet pub in Oslo city centre. Police spokesman Frank Jensen said: 'People inside began to throw chairs out of the windows and were trying to hit police. They broke windows, lamps, furniture and tables. The whole place was destroyed.'

Unfortunately, many more examples of the same sort of thing could be quoted, all of which give a bad name both to tourism and sport. They are the worst possible news for travel and tour operators, who on some occasions have reacted by excluding football supporters from trains and sea ferries. Such news items remind us of the old Spanish proverb: 'All visitors bring happiness – some by arriving; some by leaving.'

Changing patterns of holidaying

The practice of taking several shorter holidays rather than, or as well as, the traditional annual break of two weeks or more is becoming increasingly common. For various reasons the patterns of work and leisure are changing rapidly throughout Europe and the USA. People have found that holidays taken in 'week-middles' rather than at weekends mean roads, train stations, ports and air-ports are less crowded. It is also possible to have a greater choice of cheaper and more easily booked accommodation at off-peak times when there are more vacancies available. The same thinking applies to breaks taken in low season rather than in high summer. Tour operators have been quick to see the potential of this market, and most holiday companies now offer a 'winter sun' programme for the benefit of those who have finished their working life.

Nevertheless, brochures for such holidays can be rather mislead-ing. Some firms use summer photographs of crowded beaches to advertise winter holidays. They seem to suggest little difference in January between Barbados and Majorca, regardless of the fact that Barbados will be a scorching 82°F while Majorca is more likely to be a chilly 57°F. The Consumers' Association (*Holiday Which?*, November 1993) advises would-be customers to examine the over-55s brochures very carefully to get a realistic picture of destina-tions. The reality can be cardigans and cups of tea rather than suntans and swimming. Travel agents and tour operators should be quizzed ruthlessly, suggests the magazine.

'Spring breaks' or 'autumn getaways' are designed to appeal to those who are able to vary their vacation times throughout the year or take time off during the working week. Prices are usually lower when demand is less, and in fact, the whole idea of a short season into which all holidays must be compressed is becoming totally out-dated. Vacations can now be taken all year round, a sit-uation which came about partly because flights to and accommoda-tion in the Mediterranean sunbelt countries have come down in price. Even long-haul flights to genuinely hot destinations, such as Florida, Mexico and the Caribbean, can now be bought very cheaply. Taking a sunny break at times when northern regions of the world become cold is no longer the monopoly of the rich, but has recently come within the reach of masses of people.

Another reason for the extension of the short-holiday season in the colder northern European countries is the development of sun-centres, tropical worlds and other artificial, enclosed 'eco-climates' which give the illusion of enjoying sun, sea and sand far away from the chill of reality. Center Parcs, a large European concern, is the market leader in this sector and one of its slogans runs: 'Florida heat, family fun in wintery Britain!' This company will be men-tioned again in Chapter 5.

Some people do still cling to traditional holiday times, though, perhaps because it is what they have become used to or because of the demands of employers. Most often, however, it is simply the need to make family holidays coincide with the children's school vacations.

Travel motivation

The variations in holiday habits and other considerations lead on to the important question: why do tourists tour? It was noted earlier that general definitions of tourism group together all the reasons for travelling, but it is now necessary to make some distinctions.

Business or pleasure?

The principal division is between choice and necessity. There is an obvious polarisation between business and leisure traffic, which is particularly noticeable in airline operations and accommodation provision. Because of the expansion of global corporate organisations, new links established between states in Europe, the spread of democracy in eastern Europe and projects in the developing world, employees, professional workers and public servants are constantly on the move. Nowadays career patterns have expanded, and people commute between countries or continents as a matter of course.

Even this division is not clear-cut, however, because certain types of corporate hospitality breaks are related to work. In addition, the duties of cultural missions, conferences, trade fairs and working trips do usually include sightseeing excursions and entertainment evenings in their schedules. Nevertheless, a broad distinction between those trips which are undertaken mainly for the purpose of business or *mainly* for pleasure will help us to classify different sectors of tourism markets.

To get away from it all

The largest group of travellers in the holiday market is still made up of families with children, and this applies to holidays taken in the UK as well as in overseas resorts. Day-to-day family life seems to have more than its fair share of stress-inducing problems, and the routines of earning a living in commonplace surroundings can produce deadly boredom in even the most conscientious workers. Being stuck in traffic jams on the way to work, being tied to the routine of running a home or shopping in the wet and cold make people dream of getting away from it all. Mind and body need a chance to wind down: escaping to a holiday destination for rest, relaxation and above all change is a hope cherished for most of the working year by the majority of the working population. Children are promised long, sunny days on the beach, and parents hope for a chance to spend more time in each other's company and to make new friends. For all these reasons, people save their money for 11 months in order to spend it freely for two to four weeks. One leading tour operator has been quick to exploit this well-established pattern in the slogan for its TV advertising campaign: 'At Thomson we spend 52 weeks a year making your two weeks perfect!' It is to be hoped that the holiday *will* be perfect, because, after the cost of buying a house, the annual big break is probably still the most expensive single item in most family budgets.

Some light is thrown on the beliefs and intentions of holiday-makers (as they apply to the UK) by a survey conducted by Hoseasons, Britain's largest self-catering holiday operator. This research was based upon interviews with 1,000 family members and was released in January 1993. According to the survey:

- almost all the families believed that a change of scenery was as important as sunshine and luxury
- nine out of ten Britons would be taking at least one holiday in 1993–94
- more than half said that the promise of a holiday would make it easier to cope with the pressures of employment, and 76 per cent said they would return refreshed and able to work better
- 71 per cent said that the holidays they took in 1992–93 helped them to forget about money and work worries
- 95 per cent said they felt much happier after their holiday
- many said that a holiday was something to look forward to, but also that they believed it must in future be safeguarded by redundancy insurance
- the survey showed that people worked harder before their holiday – perhaps even helping indirectly to safeguard their jobs
- one family in three said that they would book earlier for their forthcoming holiday than they did the year before
- 30 per cent said they would spend more than the previous year; half would spend the same; 13 per cent said they would spend less
- when asked what they would do on holiday 96 per cent said 'relax', 64 per cent said 'would not talk about work', 58 per cent said 'stay up later', and 48 per cent said 'be more romantic'.

'To travel hopefully ...'

Young, single people contribute a great deal to the annual holiday market, and the most common reasons that they give for going on holiday are 'fun' and/or 'romance'. They too are looking for a change f scene – time out from the world of work or study. Many actively seek opportunities for participating in sport and adventure.

Considerable numbers of 17–20-year-olds and older are attracted to tourist destinations which border the Mediterranean or the warmer southern US states. Beach clubs situated in unspoilt corners of Corsica, Sardinia, Italy, Greece and Turkey are being patronised by greater numbers of youngsters each year. This may be a reaction to having spent childhood holidays on chilly shores where skies are often overcast and temperatures seldom rise above 55 degrees Fahrenheit!

Not all of the younger generation, however, are concerned with acquiring a perfect tan or finding a dream disco. A firm called Eurotrain has launched a new rail pass to eastern Europe for people aged under 26. Called the Eastbound Explorer, it covers return travel from London to seven countries, including Poland, Hungary and what was the former Czechoslovakia (from 1 January 1993 separate Czech and Slovak states came into existence). This confirms that there must be a demand for travel which allows for independence, and springs from a desire to find out about people and regions to which free access has been denied for a long time. The lifting of the Iron Curtain, the subsequent economic emergence of a number of former Eastern Bloc countries and the unification of Germany has sparked a huge interest in cities such as St Petersburg, Prague and Berlin. Demand for stays in eastern Europe was so dramatic in the season of 1993–94 that British Airways Holidays was forced to increase capacity in Russia, Slovakia and the Czech Republic. Because of the great demand for both business and leisure travel, the German airline Conti-Flug, operating from London City Airport, also started new services to Vilnius (Lithuania), Riga (Latvia) and Hamburg (Germany) in the same year.

Adventure tourism

Adventure tourism refers to holidays where a pioneering spirit and physical effort are required. Such holidays generally take the traveller to remote places with inhospitable terrain such as mountain, jungle or desert regions. Usually, the adventure tourist lives in tents or basic accommodation; there is often some kind of challenging activity such as mountaineering, trekking, canoeing or rafting. We shall discuss the impact of adventure tourism in Chapter 5.

Adventure tourists are a growing category (numbers rising at 2 per cent annually and currently estimated at eight million worldwide), and are rather hard to classify, simply because they are so individual. A large proportion are young and single, but adventure

Adventure tourism – white water rafting in Colorado, USA

tourists include people of all ages, married or single, from very varied backgrounds and professions, who want to get to know what different places and cultures are really like.

Learning holidays

Sometimes the adventures of holidaymakers are as intellectual as they are physical. There are many who have specialist interests or hobbies and would perhaps enjoy spending a fortnight on an archaeological dig, or driving a steam locomotive. Often they are looking for an active holiday which makes use of their free time to experience an alternative way of life. Some want to learn a new skill, like watercolour painting, or try their hand at a country craft, such as thatching.

In the tourism business this sector of the market is often referred to as 'self-improvement holidays', but this sounds a little too superior. In an attempt to solve the problem two words have been mixed together to form a rather clumsy new one – 'infotainment' (information/entertainment). Although this neologism (newly-invented word) describes the blend of learning and enjoyment that some look for in their ideal holiday, it is hard to imagine advertisements for infotainment holidays appearing in the travel agents' windows!

The potential clients are often tireless, enquiring travellers who demand more for their money than the old formula of 'sea, sand and snooze'. Such tourists are taking a larger share of the market now, and the reason lies perhaps in rising standards of education. In any event, their worthwhile aim is to meet individuals from other countries, or other regions of their own country, but not just waiters, cleaners, souvenir-shop attendants and couriers. They want to live and possibly work alongside people who will discuss their beliefs and exchange opinions.

Specialist tour companies have grown up to meet this demand, giving holidaymakers the opportunity for close encounters with people having very different ways of life. Some tour operators who organise the adventure holidays noted above offer the opportunity to share the day-to-day lifestyle of the hosts on an equal footing. So it is possible to go trekking with hill tribes in Thailand or stay with the primitive Kondas and Bondas tribes in India. Other options are roaming with the nomadic herdsmen of Mongolia or being guided through the forests of Zaire by Ituri pygmies. The breakthrough is that trips to exotic destinations can now provide the tourist with the chance to stay with tribal people in their homes rather than being herded and cocooned into package-tour hotels.

Some trips of this kind are organised without any commercial motive. In Jamaica for 20 years now volunteers have been running a scheme called 'Meet the People', which puts holiday-makers in touch with like-minded locals. Run with the help of the Jamaica Tourist Board, the scheme matches up people from other countries with someone of similar interests. Over the years many thousands of bus drivers, amateur cricketers, engineers, journalists, teachers and others have visited the homes of Jamaicans to enjoy their hospitality and learn about their lives and jobs.

Headline tourism

Other tourists wish to visit places which have featured in world events. So, for example, since 1963 a growing stream of sightseers has been converging on Dallas to see for themselves the spot where President Kennedy was assassinated.

The Gulf States, whose emerging tourist trade was shattered by the war of 1990, have made a strong comeback. Dubai is enjoying a major tourist boom and attracting discerning tourists. Also, in 1992, Emirates (the international airline of the United Arab Emirates) was voted best airline and presented with the Silver Globe award by *Travel Weekly*, the UK travel trade publication. That was a great achievement coming so soon after months of conflict and destruction.

Unlikely as it may seem, Lebanon was back on the tourist map by 1993. From 1975 to 1991 Beirut, the Lebanese capital, was the centre of an appalling civil war. Since the imposition of a Syrian-inspired peace, though, Beirut has started to think of itself as a travel destination once more, and package tours to this war-ravaged country are flourishing again. Apparently there is no shortage of those who want to see with their own eyes the locations they have only previously been able to glimpse on television.

The most dramatic transformation of a trouble-ridden country into a wonderful tourist venue is perhaps South Africa. For years the country was avoided by the world's tourism industry because of its apartheid policies and the frequent outbreaks of violence which made headline news and marred its image. Due to long-awaited political changes, however, South Africa has now become a democracy, and international sanctions have been lifted. The natural beauty of the country, with some of the finest safari territory, beaches and mountain scenery in the world, has been carefully conserved, and in addition there are all the comforts and conveniences that tourists expect from a developed state. Modern, bustling cities that can boast sophisticated night-life, luxury hotels, good food and fine wine are served by excellent roads and up-to-date transport. This adds up to a combination which is ideal for tourism, and has led to South Africa being described as 'a Third World country with a First World infrastructure' (from 'Jungle Belles' in 'Night and Day', the *Mail on Sunday Review* by Anthony Haden-Guest, 5 December 1993).

What is most important now to the country's citizens is the proper management necessary to ensure that tourism provides jobs and foreign currency without the divisive and damaging effects that can be seen in other parts of the world. Over the next few years tour operators will be looking for signs that the end of the hatred and poverty that apartheid promoted has led to a prosperous and happy state where visitors can take racial harmony for granted. It is in the interest of everyone to protect this newly found peace in South Africa in order to create a better standard of living for black and white alike.

Cultural tourism

Historical sites like Rome, Athens, Carthage and the pyramids of Egypt have been drawing cultural tourists for many hundreds of years. Now the opportunity to view these and other relics of the ancient world at first hand has been thrown open to the greatly increased numbers of people wishing to complement their education and enlarge their experience.

Places of special interest such as galleries, museums and

cathedrals have gained a greater following in recent years. There are also those who will travel thousands of miles to attend outstanding events. Ballets in Beijing, theatrical performances at Oberammergau, pop concerts in Venice and seasons of Shakespeare in Stratford are all attended (and often made viable) by lovers of the performing arts, many of whom have saved for years to enjoy their experience of a lifetime. An example of the financial support given by visitors to showbusiness may be seen in a report issued in 1993 by the London Tourist Board. The report found that:

- tourists now account for two-fifths of all theatre tickets bought in London and a quarter of the capital's taxi fares
- overseas visitors spent £3.7 billion in London in 1992
- in all, London received 15.5 million visitors in 1992: half of these came for a holiday, about a quarter came on business and the rest were visiting friends and relatives.

Visits to friends and relatives (VFR)

World populations have been kept on the move for a long time because of constant emigration and immigration. The European empires of previous centuries gave rise to a two-way traffic from the home countries to the distant lands where their dominions, colonies, dependencies and so on were located. Relatives travelled to join or revisit their families, and regular sea services were developed between Britain and Canada, Europe and America, Spain and South America and Holland and the Dutch East Indies (just to give a few instances). Great shipping lines prospered on the proceeds of this trade and, in the post-colonial era, the airline companies still do good business maintaining these well-established intercontinental links.

After the Second World War immigration to Europe increased greatly. Families from the Indian sub-continent, the West Indies, Africa, Hong Kong and other places came to share in European prosperity, and in return brought the enriching influence of their own culture. They were not tourists, because they had come to settle, and they often left behind friends and relatives. With the coming of greater affluence, many now pay regular visits to their former homelands to renew family ties. Others who were born in European countries make journeys or pilgrimages to revitalise religious faith or discover cultural identity. Tour operators and travel agents refer to this as *ethnic tourism*.

Within the domestic tourism trade of most countries, VFR account for a huge volume of business, in longer breaks as well as day trips. This is especially true during the traditional summer vacation periods and at such times as bank holidays and Christmas. Parties comprising extended families are also responsible for large numbers of bookings both at home and abroad. There is no doubt that from a social and cultural point of view VFR may be considered one of the most important sectors of the industry.

Tourism for health and fitness activities

This type of tourism is one of the oldest reasons for travelling. To take a journey for the sake of one's health has been a cure prescribed for hundreds of years, and the habit still continues. British seaside resorts came into being because it was believed that sea water and sea air had almost miraculous properties. Convalescent, retirement and rest homes were located by the sea, though this practice fell out of favour to some extent as the smoke pollution in and around cities was lessened by various Acts of Parliament. Our more health-conscious European neighbours have never lost interest in the restorative properties of natural cures. In France, for instance, there are 21 centres offering thalasso therapy, which are worth more than £35 million to the French leisure and tourist industry. Thalasso comes from the Greek word *thalassa* meaning sea water, and it is a therapy for the prevention or treatment of physical and neurological disorders using the sea's muds, weeds, sands, water and climate. (See Case study 2 on Biarritz, p. 149.)

The British have been aware of the healing power of certain types of mineral water for centuries, so spas and hydros have enjoyed enormous popularity. There is an organisation known as the British Spas Federation which promotes Britain's 12 spa towns as tourist attractions. Even if taking the waters is no longer fashionable, these charming places have pleasant architecture, stand in lovely countryside and rank high as tourist attractions. The better-known ones – Bath, Harrogate and Cheltenham – still flourish in a limited way as cure centres. The Pump Room Museum in Bath claimed, perhaps rather optimistically, that the waters in its Pump Room, and the Turkish baths in the Assembly Rooms would 'ease away aches and pains with a water treatment as efficient as anything modern medicine can provide'. The ancient spring at Bath still flows, and visitors to the Pump Room are given a glass of the 'wonder water' if they request it. Droitwich Spa, a small town in Worcestershire, is an interesting case. It has the only working brine spa in the UK and has recently insisted on having the title 'spa' added to its name. This is partly as a tribute to its long history as a spa town, and partly in the hope that the genuine medical worth of its treatments will be recognised.

The Pump Room in Bath c. 1870

On the whole, though, spa towns in Britain are simply inland resorts which are visited for relaxation and fun. Their modern clientele is made up of 'tourists rather than curists'. There used to be exclusive establishments called health farms, but so many jokes were made about the name and the strict dietary regimes that were followed there that an image change was essential. Now there are 'health and fitness centres', often located in former stately homes or high-quality, purpose-built premises which offer holidays with an up-to-date emphasis on such matters as diet, exercise and relaxation therapies.

Most international-class hotels have professionally staffed gymnasia, swimming pools, and squash and tennis courts as a matter of routine and all offer a lean-cuisine type of menu. Health consciousness is big business and plays an important part in the marketing of accommodation and attractions, so the topic will be dealt with more fully in Case Study 2.

Tourism for purposes of sport

Earlier in this chapter an example was given of the bad publicity that football fans can attract. It is important to remember, though, that for every hooligan there are a thousand genuine lovers of the game who gain much from their travels to other countries and are no trouble to their hosts.

Soccer is not the only game that has a wide following. Most sports, in fact, generate huge tourist activity. One has only to think of the international crowds drawn to the Wimbledon Lawn Tennis Championships, or the great gatherings at Ascot and Goodwood. There are too many sporting activities to mention individually, but a glance at a calendar for the sporting year will show a tremendous variety of games and locations. Golf championships, for instance, move to warm countries in winter, so the Madeira Island Open, the Johnnie Walker Classic in Singapore and the Dubai Desert Classic mean an influx of players and followers to swell the tourist trade in January and February. Also during the winter months there are ideal conditions for seasonal sports in colder countries. January sees, for example, the Bobsleigh European Championships at St Moritz (Switzerland) and the Bobsleigh World Cup at Cortina (Italy). The European Figure Skating Championship (Helsinki, Finland) and the Men's World Cup for Skiing (Kitzbühel, Austria) are held in the same month.

Each week of each month of every year is filled with events ranging from motor racing to rugby. Somewhere around the globe, international crowds are always flocking to watch badminton and boxing, windsurfing and wrestling, cricket and cycling. Sport is inextricably mixed with travel, and the revenue generated by this type of tourism supports or contributes greatly towards the economies of many countries.

Some idea of the importance of sport in today's world may be given by examining the bid which Manchester made to host the Olympic Games in the year 2000. The Games which, along with the Winter Olympics, are held every four years, represent the summit of athletic and sporting activity. They bring great prestige and (sometimes) prosperity to the places where they are held. Manchester's bid proved, sadly, to be unsuccessful when the honour of hosting the Games went to Sydney, Australia. Nevertheless, because of the thorough preparations made over a period of eight years, Sir Robert Scott, chairman of the Olympic bid, has already been able to make plans for Manchester to become the venue for the next Commonwealth Games in 2002 and perhaps even to capture the 2004 Olympics. The spin-off benefits for Manchester of the 1993 bid have already included:

- a £235 million development around Victoria Station
- an 18,000-seat Olympic arena costing £50 million to be part of a complex which will include a hotel, a cinema, shops and offices, as well as new roads
- a £35.5 million grant from the Government towards the project, under its programme to regenerate inner cities

- more impetus given to the completion of the splendid new Manchester Airport terminal.

Besides the victorious Sydney, other cities – Beijing, Istanbul, Milan, Berlin, Brasilia and Tashkent among them – all made similar Olympic preparations. It does not take much imagination to appreciate the vast sums of money generated, the great boost given to employment and the future facilities that will be provided because of these charismatic international athletics.

To get some much-needed knowledge

This final lighthearted section in answer to the question 'why do tourists tour?' is prompted by the howlers that appeared in answer to a series of questions set by the London Tourist Board in 1993 to find out what tourists know about London.

The questionnaire was answered by more than 2,000 foreign visitors and 234 from Britain who visited the tourist information centre close to London's Victoria Station. Some of them believed that:

- Big Ben is a statue of a famous general
- Beefeaters is the name of the England rugby team
- Knightsbridge spans the Thames
- Baker Street is where the Great Fire of London started
- Petticoat Lane is the lingerie centre of London
- Madame Tussaud's is a designer-clothes store.

Only 6 per cent of those who took part got all the questions right and, of these, 64 per cent were overseas visitors. It seems as though a little more travel and tourism would be good for us all!

The changing tourist map

Scenarios for developing leisure and business travel provision are found most usually in the affluent industrialised communities of northern Europe, the northern states of the USA, the prosperous parts of the Far East and the Middle East. These areas are sometimes described as *the tourism-generating regions*. Locations with a warm climate and picturesque scenery are usually regarded as *tourism-receiving regions*.

It must be emphasised that the above remarks are generalisations based on past experience of holidaymaking patterns. Tourism objectives and tourist destinations are as varied as the individuals who are shopping for holidays and business travel, so fashions come and go in this trade as in any other. An example of this is the massive rush to Spain and the Balearics of 1993–94. Since their heyday in the 1960s and '70s 'Costa' holidays had been rather out of favour with the British public. However, the demand for 1994 was so great that Thomson, the biggest UK tour operator, bought an extra 250,000 beds at Spanish resorts on top of the one million they had already booked. After a decade in which British holiday-makers experimented with Florida, Tenerife, Tunisia, Greece, Turkey and the Far East, many of the 14.85 million who go abroad each year opted again for two weeks in the Spanish sun at an average price of £350 half-board.

Over the last decade one of the most remarkable tourism developments has been the growth of winter sports holidays. For a hundred years skiing, skating and tobogganing in the exclusive resorts of Switzerland and Italy were the preserve of the rich and leisured. Now, because of longer and more flexible holidays as well as increasingly cheap travel, skiing holidays are well within the reach of ordinary families. In addition to the well-established resorts of Austria and France, new venues are appearing all round the globe at prices which are far cheaper than those in the European Alps. At a price of £399 a Californian skiing holiday, inclusive of air travel, hotel and car hire, is easily affordable for many British enthusiasts. Canada also offers many bargains to European skiers and has developed a flourishing winter tourist trade by marketing its great asset of guaranteed, good quality snow. Even lower prices make winter sports holidays in eastern European countries very attractive. A week of skiing in Bulgaria or Romania, for instance, can cost as little as £129. Norway is now advertising itself as 'The ideal winter playground' and has more than a hundred ski resorts, some with prices starting at £149. There are many other emerging destinations, but these few examples make the point that the tourist demand for affordable winter holidays is opening up regions which even five years ago would never have considered the possibility.

World events and national crises ensure that tourism remains a dynamic, not to say volatile industry, and changes appear from year to year. Some upsets are blips which last only a season or two. Others cause radical changes and affect the fates of governments and national economies.

The developed world has its problems and setbacks from time to time. Increases in fuel costs, freak weather, recessions and slumps all cause variations in the patterns of both tourism-generating and tourism-receiving. The developing world continues to make progress in establishing its own manufacturing industries and increasing its trading capacities. However, for the past few decades the assumption that continuing industrial and economic growth is always a good thing has been questioned. The developing world is now beginning to decide for itself what goals its tourism philosophies should aim for. The underdeveloped or Third World is making steady progress towards self-sufficiency through international aid and improved education, but it does not welcome overexploitation. Decolonisation and the swing to self-determination have led to more positive attitudes. Among poorer tourist-receiving areas which are just emerging, there is an atmosphere of great caution and a conviction that resources must be shared fairly.

Although the Cold War has ended, there are many flash points around the globe that threaten regional or international stability. The influential journal *Jane's Defence Weekly* in its yearly survey (1993) identifies 26 wars or insurrections, 23 areas of potential conflict and 24 areas of tension; the alphabet of unrest ranges from Afghanistan to Zaire. *Jane's* publisher, Paul Beaver, said: 'We continue to live in the most dangerous decade of this century, and possibly ever.'

All of this brings great uncertainty to the minds of tourists and tourism providers alike. For some aspects of the subject, therefore, only estimates rather than hard statistics can be gathered. Some of these matters will be looked at further in later chapters.

Assignment: *The choice of a holiday*

In the section on travel motivation 'To get away from it all' it was noted that the biggest sector of the recreational holiday market is made up of family groups. Consider the following situation:

The Storey family consists of John, aged 36, his wife Sandra, aged 35, their eldest child, Martin, aged 15, their daughter Lucy, aged 10 and their youngest child, Karen, who is aged 4.

During January and February they have been thinking about their annual summer holiday, which, as always for them, will be a fortnight in length and has to fit in with the children's school holidays in July and August. They have been saving for a year and have decided to take all the children abroad together for the first time. John has quite a stressful office job and Sandra finds looking after the home and family a full-time occupation, so they are both looking forward to relaxing and having a good time. In addition they want the children to be happily entertained whilst being safely and actively occupied. After glancing at some holiday brochures and much discussion they have narrowed down their choice to three possible holidays, all of which will, they believe, cost the same amount within a few pounds. These are the alternatives they are considering:

Holiday 1 would be a package from the brochure of a large tour operator. It offers 14 days half-board in a large high-rise, three-star hotel on the Costa del Sol. The hotel has private gardens and is close to the beach. The overall cost includes air fares and transfers from Malaga Airport to the hotel.

Holiday 2 would be a camping holiday in Provence. The site, in a region of great natural beauty, is within comfortable driving distance of some interesting old towns and sites of historic interest. It is well kept and well equipped, with an excellent toilet/shower block, restaurant, swimming pool and sports facilities. All the tents are provided with beds, cookers and a refrigerator. The Storeys would travel in their own car.

Holiday 3 is located in a corner of one of the larger Greek islands. Accommodation is self-catering and consists of a spacious, clean, two-bedroomed flat in a purpose-built apartment complex within reasonable walking distance of a former fishing village which has become a small tourist resort. There are facilities for most types of water sports and some clean beaches. The Storeys would fly by scheduled service to a main airport and would then have a two-and-a-half hour coach journey to their final destination.

The Storeys ask you which holiday you think would be the most enjoyable for all the family. Working in three groups, examine each alternative in detail. Prepare a presentation, using visual aids, to promote and sell the holiday which you chose. To do this, you will have to obtain a good selection of different brochures either from travel agents or by writing for information to addresses which you will find in newspaper advertisements. Find holidays which cost approximately the same and cost out any extra expenses which the Storey family will have to meet.

There are many other questions which you will have to answer when considering each holiday, for example:

- Are the tour operators/travel agents fully bonded?
- What, exactly, does the holiday insurance offered by the tour operator/travel agent cover? Is extra insurance advisable?
- Which type of passport is necessary on each holiday?
- What are the relative advantages and disadvantages of travelling by car or by air with three children of different ages?

- If the family decide on the French camping holiday, which is the best method of getting across the Channel with regard to cost and convenience? What are the best and the worst times to travel on the main roads of France? All the French *autoroutes* are toll roads. Do they know that the cost of driving a standard family car from the Channel ports to the South of France is about £42 each way?
- Do any of the charter airlines make special provision for children who have not flown before?
- Do any of the hotels listed in the Spanish packages have special facilities for children (special menus, supervised playgroups, separate pools for young children, baby sitting arrangements, etc.)?
- How do Spanish three-star ratings compare to their British equivalents? Do any of them offer 'free extras' or 'welcome packages'?
- Do any tour operators offer 'first two children free'?
- Do the hotel gardens adjoin the beach, or are they separated by a busy road?
- Will the children have to climb many flights of stairs every time they come into or leave the hotel bedroom? Are there adequate arrangements for child safety in and around the hotel?
- Is the apartment complex in the Greek alternative set in a quiet or lively location?
- Are the beaches mentioned in the Spanish and Greek packages sandy or stony?
- What are the seasonal average hours of sunshine and maximum temperatures for each location?

2   How did it all begin?

It is surprising that the reasons for travelling in the past were so similar to current factors of tourist motivation. To understand fully the importance of tourism it is necessary to glance at its long and fascinating history, and realise that in a sense all tourist journeys are voyages of discovery or pilgrimages. The enterprising spirit that today prompts people to travel long distances, whether to conduct business deals or to see the world with their own eyes, is essentially the same as that which led the people of ancient civilisations to explore the lands and seas of their world.

The ancient world

People have always wanted to move further and faster. It is believed that as early as 3000 BC ships had been designed that would cross open water with safety and follow a predictable course. The remains of solid-wheeled wagons dating back to 2500 BC have been unearthed by archaeologists excavating the sites of Sumerian cities in northern Mesopotamia. There is evidence that the Egyptians used horses as far back as 2300 BC, and that by 1600 BC they had devised light chariots with spoked wheels. From paintings on the walls of their tombs it appears that they too travelled for pleasure and recreation – sometimes just for a change of scene or to pay visits to friends.

The adventurers, traders, fishermen and colonists who between 800 and 500 BC sailed from the mainland of Greece and Asia Minor were tourists, in the sense that their journeys were always in a circuit. Greek businessmen travelled from the Crimea to France and Ireland looking for trade. They also brought back carpets from Carthage, ivory from Africa, glass from Egypt and perfumes from Arabia. However far they wandered, though, they had the intention of returning home to sell their goods, share their knowledge and invest their profits. It was their curiosity that discovered the main features of the Mediterranean and the routes out of it. Around 325 BC, for instance, there was a Greek colony at Massilia (the modern Marseilles) from where Pytheas, a trader, set sail to explore the coasts of Spain and France. He found his way through the Strait of Gibraltar, and it is believed that he actually sailed round Britain and up towards the Baltic before returning home.

At about the same time, in 332 BC, Alexander the Great marched from Greece through Syria, Persia and the Khyber Pass to discover a land route to India. This route was followed in 290 BC by the scholar Megasthenes, who had a happy holiday in the valley of the Ganges, and wrote an account of the area and its people to take home with him. Just like any tourist of today, he complained about the weather when he was caught in the monsoon rains! Herodotus, the first travel writer and professional tourist, was also a Greek. He was born into a rich and well-educated family at the beginning of the fifth century BC and devoted his life to touring around the Mediterranean and Asia Minor. His work provides us with valuable information about the ancient world, but more importantly it shows us that human nature was much the same 2,500 years ago.

The luxury goods, such as spices and silks, which could be imported from Asia and the countries around the Indian Ocean, were just as popular with the Romans when their empire succeeded that of the Greeks, and they travelled even further. It is well known that Julius Caesar first visited Britain in 55 and 54 BC. Less known, however, is that by the first century AD the Romans had found a way to China by travelling east of the Euphrates and on through Central Asia. Like the Greeks, the Romans were determined colonisers and left their mark throughout the world as they extended their frontiers. The urge to travel inevitably created a demand for fresh places to be explored, and so to the development of the means of getting there and back.

In the ancient world, conquest and trade were the prime reasons for travelling. We have only to look at the history of Rome to realise that their famous road-building, their improvements to horse-drawn vehicles, and all their refinements in navigation and the building of ships came about because of their military ambitions. The power of the Roman Empire spread rapidly over what is now Europe as well as around the Mediterranean and into Asia Minor. Behind the tramping legions and the chariots of their commanders came the administrators, diplomats and dealers looking for new realms to control and new markets to develop. These pioneers were followed by what we should now recognise as tourists – seekers after new knowledge, keen observers of the lives and customs of different peoples, and those who wished to admire natural marvels and geographical features.

The Middle Ages

In the fifth century AD the overthrow of the western half of the Roman Empire by the barbarian hordes of the Goths, Vandals and Lombards set back the process of discovery which was helping the spread of learning and knowledge. Travel and tourism can only be developed where there is order, civilisation and good lines of communication.

Fortunately a Greek Christian world survived until 1453. This was ruled by the Eastern Roman or Byzantine emperors from their capital at Constantinople. There the Roman achievements in government and technology were preserved and developed alongside the Greek spirit of enquiry and respect for learning. After the stages of discovery and colonisation, the next stage was the sharing of cultures. It was tourism and peaceful travel that assisted this transfer and cross-fertilisation of languages, religions, principles of law and government, and the application of scientific knowledge to the needs of society.

The rise of Islam in the seventh and eighth centuries opened up fresh perspectives in art and science, when this vital and vigorous new civilisation gained control over the southern and eastern coasts of the Mediterranean. In fact, the Arab Empire, which was at the height of its power in about AD 1000, reached from the Atlantic coast to the far end of the Indian Ocean. Its learned men admired the work of the Greeks and developed their scientific investigations into the physical nature of the world. The administration of this vast domain and the custom of making a pilgrimage to Mecca gave rise to a tremendous volume of travel, together with a valuable interchange of ideas and knowledge. The writings of Arab scholars such as Ibn Khordadbeh (AD 850) and Ibn Haukal (AD 998) detailed the trade routes and the geography of their great empire. Parts of what is now Spain came under the control of the Moors during this period, and to the present day tourists flock in their millions to admire the legacy of art and architecture which they left behind.

The Crusades (1095–1291) were a vain attempt to recover the Christian Holy Land from the Muslems. With hindsight, we can see that this was a misguided series of campaigns, which was to create unnecessary hostility and bloodshed, as well as disrupting overland trading routes with the East. On the positive side, it must be admitted that many people in western Europe gained a much better knowledge of the eastern Mediterranean and its inhabitants as a result of their military travels. On the other hand, when the men of Christendom saw the rich commodities such as silks, spices, precious stones, porcelain and tapestries that were pouring into

Muslem lands from the Orient, they felt the need to have access to these luxuries themselves. Unfortunately for them the Muslems were firmly established at the geographical crossroads between East and West and maintained such a barrier to travel that only a rare few European travellers such as Marco Polo, in the second half of the thirteenth century, succeeded in penetrating as far as China. The city-states of Venice and Genoa did have a trading agreement whereby they bought Eastern goods from the Muslem merchants and sold them on to the rest of Europe at a handsome profit. This generated a great deal of travel and prosperity around the north of Italy, but it also set men of wealth and vision dreaming of an ocean route to the East which would by-pass the Mediterranean and its Muslem-held shores.

The Renaissance

In the fourteenth century the eventual defeat of the Moors in Europe gave rise to two powerful nations, Spain and Portugal. These states occupied the Iberian peninsula, and as they wished to increase their wealth and influence by exploration and trade – even possibly by finding the elusive direct sea route to the East – it was natural that they should venture into the mysterious Atlantic Ocean that washed their shores. The results of this policy are well known, and every tourist who has set foot in the West Indies has to acknowledge a debt to Columbus (1451–1506), whose famous voyage which began in Portugal ended in the discovery of whole 'new' worlds.

There followed the golden age of exploration, a time when monarchs vied with one another to lay hands on the treasures of territories across the western ocean and around the western coast of Africa. Navigators were in great demand. Henry VII of England, for instance, employed the services of Anglo-Italian John Cabot (1450–98). When the latter set sail, accompanied by his son Sebastian, from Bristol on 2 May 1497, he carried letters from the king authorising him 'to seek out, discover and find all hitherto unknown lands'. Although this was rather a tall order, Cabot did reach Cape Breton Island at the mouth of the St Lawrence River in North America and went on to rediscover Newfoundland.

After the upset and confusion caused by the barbarian invasions, there had been long power-struggles between popes and emperors, and battles for supremacy between feudal kings and their rival nobles. War followed war, each one bringing more misery and anarchy. Eventually some kind of order returned to Europe, and by the fifteenth century, powerful nation-states had grown up to create the sort of stability that would encourage travel and trade, and towns and centres of learning began to flourish. All through the so-called Dark Ages the medieval universities had kept alive some spirit of civilisation and preserved the learning and literature of Greece and Rome. As early as 1167 there had been a two-way traffic of what we would now call educational tourism between Paris and Oxford. Scholars were attracted by the fame of great international teachers, and would travel enormous distances to hear them and discuss new ideas. When, for instance, there was a dispute between Oxford academics in 1209, a break-away group of intellectuals moved to Cambridge to found another centre of learning. The arrival there in 1510 of the great Dutch scholar, Erasmus, rapidly increased the popularity of that university.

In the Iberian peninsula the Muslims had established influential universities which had at first been open only to followers of Islam and Jews, but as the reconquest proceeded, the universities fell into Christian hands, even though some of their original scholars stayed on to teach. Salamanca was the capital city of a Spanish province on the River Tormes and a university was founded there in 1218 by Alfonso IX of Leon. It became widely known under Alfonso X and much more so later, when Columbus gave lectures there on his discoveries. Padua had always been famous for its teachers, but even more students made the difficult journey over the Alps during the professorship of Galileo (1592–1610). The university at Bologna, which had been founded in 1088, and where Master Rolandino taught Roman law in the thirteenth century, made a unique contribution to the spread of knowledge, the sharing of talent and the establishment of order. Many more instances could be given of towns which drew travellers over hundreds or even thousands of miles of difficult terrain to become part of what was known as the Renaissance, that is, the rebirth of thought and learning.

This great movement came to a head in the fourteenth and fifteenth centuries in Italy, and its effects spread slowly throughout France, Spain, the Netherlands, Germany and England. The Renaissance encouraged people to shake off the narrow and rigid medieval restraints on thinking for themselves and focused their attention on the world around them. When printing was developed at the end of the fifteenth century, there was a flood of information and ideas which became a part of everyday life, so that the urge to travel, learn and discover received a tremendous boost. Students, artists, herbalists and antiquaries began to outnumber the hordes of wandering mercenary soldiers and vagabonds who had taken to the roads after the end of feudal wars.

Pilgrimages

To this surge of travel there were added bands of pilgrims and church officials. Journeys for religious reasons began after the spread of Christianity in Europe and the founding of Islam in the East. Roads and bridges were built and maintained by the Catholic Church to speed travel throughout the Holy Roman Empire. The first inns developed from religious hostels and those sections of abbeys where free food and shelter were handed out to help pious travellers on their way.

Turkish Muslims had throughout their country a system of *khans*, which were resting places for travellers. Many of these were magnificent stone buildings standing close to a mosque, though some were more like stables with a sleeping-shelf around the wall. These charitable lodgings were provided by the rich as good works with which to please Allah, but all were open to Muslem, Christian and Jew alike. Even the simplest *khans* offered, without charge, clean accommodation, water for washing, and, to eat, porridge with meat in it followed by a dessert of bread and honey. Religious tourism continues to the present day and accounts for an enormous volume of travel worldwide. There are, in fact, still a few hospitable places left where no charge is made to devout travellers for their board and lodging.

When more peaceful times returned to the Middle East in the fourteenth and fifteenth centuries, the ideal of every Christian was to atone for the misbehaviour of a year or more by making a journey to the Holy Land. There was even a regular service of 'Pilgrim galleys', which in the fifteenth and sixteenth centuries did the journey from Venice to Jaffa in about five weeks – storms, pirates and disease permitting! Only the very rich could afford to go as far as the Holy Sepulchre in Jerusalem. Others would make the shorter journey to Rome or to one of the many shrines that were spread around Europe – usually situated in magnificent cathedrals that the Church had built to commemorate saints and martyrs.

For 300 years Canterbury was one of the most famous shrines in Christendom and was a religious centre full of ritual and ceremony. All nationalities flocked there to crowd its streets, inns and hostels. By the time that Geoffrey Chaucer (*c.* 1343–1400) wrote his famous *Canterbury Tales* it is clear that pilgrimages had become something of an excuse for holiday trips and a change of company. We must remember that in the Middle Ages there were about 115 holy days a year – and holy days gave us our word 'holidays'. The fairs and entertainments that surrounded shrines prospered, and even the religious authorities were not above selling badges, dubious holy relics and bottles of holy water. The same instinct is seen today in tourists who would not think of returning from holiday without bringing souvenirs to show that they had actually 'been there; done that'.

Motives varied. Some women went to holy places in search of fertility, other people went to find cures for illnesses, and some simply travelled to be near the source of their faith. The diarist John Evelyn records that in the year 1600, 25,000 women visitors and 44,000 men were registered at the Pilgrims' Hospice of the Holy Trinity at Rome. Pilgrims are still big business to this day, and many journey, though much more comfortably and rapidly, to Lourdes or Loreto, Rome or Mecca for the same reasons as their remote ancestors.

The roads

Whatever the reasons for travelling in distant days, one thing is sure: there were very few who looked forward to actually being on the road. 'A journey is a fragment of hell', wrote the Turkish traveller, Awliyai Efendi (1611–79), and most travellers up to the eighteenth century would have agreed with him.

The well-engineered roads which the Romans had built across Europe fell rapidly into neglect after their empire collapsed. This was due partly to the loss of the constructional skills which they had brought with them, but also because in feudal times it was to the advantage of powerful nobles to live in strongholds which were hard to find and difficult to approach. For centuries there was no central authority apart from the Church to look after the roads, and throughout Europe, after the Reformation, few surfaces were paved outside cities or towns. Rain always caused trouble. The dust which had choked the lungs and irritated the eyes of summer travellers was turned into mire, an unpleasant combination of mud, rotting leaves and the droppings of all the animals that had been ridden or driven along the route. No one walked in it through choice! Even horses had to travel in single file, stumbling from one water-filled hole to the next. Because of the lack of engineering skills gradients were often steep and, when wet, became slippery with mud and loose stones.

Most old roads followed bare, high ground to give fewer opportunities for brigands to swoop down from above or hide in the thick foliage of valleys. Another reason for avoiding low ground was the nuisance of flooding. Bridges were only built on major roads, and smaller roads had to be crossed by fords, which in winter were impassable for weeks on end. Low-lying areas were usually crossed by causeways, but after heavy rain these became covered with surface water. As the road thus became invisible, the traveller was never sure whether he was safely moving along, with the ground just a foot below him, or about to slither into cold, muddy depths of 10 or 12 feet – little wonder that the winter tourist season was rather quiet! Add to this the fact that there were no street lights, milestones or road signs and only a very few primitive inns, and we can see why the hire of a trustworthy guide was essential.

The history of tourism is closely linked to the development of transportation technology, and A. Babeau, in his book *Les Voyageurs en France depuis la Renaissance jusqu'à la Révolution* (written in 1885) says that travel may be divided into three ages: the age of the horse, the carriage and the railway. Certainly until roads were properly surfaced the horse was the only way of travelling with any reasonable speed. Goods were usually carried by pack animals or on crude carts. By the fifteenth century there were clumsy coaches and unsprung, lumbering stage-waggons, but without good roads these were of very limited use. Those who could afford neither horse nor a place in a cart travelled on foot and carried any goods or possessions on their backs. Nevertheless, pleasant or unpleasant, comfortable or uncomfortable, some journeys had to be made. The settled nation-states of the sixteenth century had strong rulers who were determined to add to the wealth and power of their countries by trade and travel. There arose as a result the notion of the King's Highway – a network of passable roads which would make possible the administration of justice and the distribution of goods.

The discomforts of travel

At this time few people were interested in discovering and enjoying the beauties of nature; it is the growth in the size of towns that has made the remoter aspects of nature now seem so desirable. Before the Industrial Revolution the average person was surrounded by just about as much nature as he or she could stand – it was only the lessening of the dangers and discomforts of travel that gave people the chance to find pleasure in getting out and about and taking holidays away from home.

Accommodation for travellers was such that most people approached the prospect of a necessary journey with fear and foreboding. An account of a Polish inn by Charles Ogier in his book *Ephemerides* (written in 1656) shows why:

> The sleeping room was something between a stable and a subterranean furnace. Six soldiers lay on the ground as if dead; the peasant-tenant, his wife, children and servants, lay on benches round the walls with cover-

ings of straw and feathers. In one corner slept a Calvinist, a baron's secretary; in another, on the peasant's straw pallet, an ambassador's chaplain, a Roman Catholic; and between the two, to save each it seemed, from the heels of the other, was lying a huge Tartar, a captain in the Polish army, who had made up a bed of hay for himself. About the room were dogs, geese, pigs, fowls; while the corner by the oven was conceded to a woman who had just given birth to a child. The baby cried, the mother moaned, the tired servants and soldiers snored; and early in the morning the writer rose from the shelf he was sharing with some leggings, spurs and muskets, and escaped.

A book of advice to tourists issued by 'Gruberus' (a Latin pen-name for a typical guide-book writer) in the seventeenth century offers some practical tips:

Line your doublet with taffetie; taffetie is lice-proof.

Never journey without something to eat in your pocket, if only to throw to dogs when attacked by them.

When going by coach, avoid women, especially old women; they always want the best places.

At sea remove your spurs; sailors make a point of stealing them from those who are being sea-sick. Keep your distance from them in any case; they are covered with vermin.

In an inn-bedroom which contains big pictures, look behind the latter to see they do not conceal a secret door or a window.

Women should not travel at all and married men not much.

Apart from minor miseries like these, travellers ran risks from war, famine, plague, fires, revolutions, sieges and robbers. Anyone who ventured abroad needed a well-filled purse because the costs of touring were also high in financial terms. In those distant days of few laws and many national boundaries there were petty tyrants, unscrupulous hosts, dishonest traders and corrupt officials waiting to fleece the passing stranger. The charges for fares, food, lodgings, passports, tolls and so on were often varied to match the appearance and apparent prosperity of the visitor.

Waterways and coaches

Wherever possible those who had to travel made great use of inland waterways or were carried in small vessels that hugged the coasts. The Thames, the Seine, the Rhine and the Danube, to mention but a few, were vitally important as arteries of trade and tourism, and all rivers of navigable size were frequented by boats which carried both cargo and passengers. Water transport, though, was slow and often dangerous, and of course rivers and coastal waters could not reach all destinations.

The age of the carriage was rather slow in arriving, but with the coming of settled monarchies and the rise of national trade more wheeled vehicles thronged the roads. There was another problem: even though by the end of the seventeenth century the technology existed to construct lighter, faster vehicles, carts and coaches remained heavy and slow because they had to have the strength to travel the rutted, rocky roads of the time. As a result of the terrible condition of roads all over Europe, horses lamed by loose stones, breakdowns and the overturning of coaches were common events, and even if such accidents did not happen, many passengers were literally road-sick because of the constant swaying and jolting. Coaches and waggons usually travelled only in spring, summer and early autumn, and then not often on Sundays.

This situation persisted for a surprisingly long time in England and even as late as 1768, Arthur Young, a famous traveller and agriculturalist, complained about the poor state of the roads in his book *Six Weeks' Tour Through the Southern Counties*. Of the road from Witney to Northleach in Oxfordshire he wrote:

> So bad, it is a scandal to the county. They mend and make with nothing but the stone which forms the under-stratum all over the country. This stone, which rises in vast flakes, would make an admirable foundation for a surface of gravel; but by using it alone, and in pieces as large as one's head, the road is rendered most execrable.

Under these conditions, even one's own country must have seemed very large and strange, and most people – even many of those with the means to travel – spent their lives as in medieval times, without ever going more than 10 miles from their own door. As European states traded more with each other, all who hoped to govern or deal in commodities had to have a wider knowledge of the world. The upper classes, therefore began to adopt the practice of sending their sons (and sometimes even their daughters) abroad to acquire information and an appreciation of art and architecture, and business and culture. By about 1750 this had become a recognised custom and was known as the 'grand tour'. It was by no means just a British institution. Continental countries, including Poland, Russia and Scandanavia all had their own grand tours, whilst the Spanish and the Portuguese made grand tours to their exotic overseas dominions. Travelling, however, was so uncomfortable that it still took tremendous wealth, great courage and genuine interest to undertake long journeys abroad.

At the end of the eighteenth and the beginning of the nineteenth centuries, the long series of Napoleonic Wars that ravaged Europe meant that the continent was closed to grand tourists. Touring in Britain became more popular as a result, and partly because of this, efforts had to be made to improve the state of roads in England. Local authorities were given the power to demand tolls from road users in order to maintain the highways. To halt traffic so that money might be collected, turnpikes were set up. These were originally barriers of pikes (long spears) which spanned the road and could be turned on a pivot to allow vehicles past. By the middle of the eighteenth century these fearsome devices had been replaced by large toll-gates topped by spikes, but the word 'turnpike' survived – and still does in America where it denotes a main toll-road.

In spite of this system journeys remained painfully slow, and a glance at some of the times taken in the middle of the eighteenth century between London and some other British cities illustrates why few people took the trouble to get to know their own country, let alone venture abroad:

Table 3 Typical journey times in the mid-1700s	
London –	Days
Dover	2
Manchester	4 ½
Birmingham	2 ½
Exeter	6
Edinburgh	12

Thomas Telford (1757–1834) and John McAdam (1756–1836) were the two brilliant civil engineers who transformed the roads of Britain. They followed the Roman principle of making a bed of earth and laying graded layers of smaller and smaller stones over the top, but instead of a stone slab surface, they used a wearing surface of gravel. McAdam also introduced the rounded surface or camber into road-building. This innovation meant that rainwater ran down into stone gutters and was carried away. Thomas De Quincey (1785–1859) wrote in 1849 in his book *The English Mail Coach*:

All the roads of England were re-modelled upon the principles of Roman science. From mere beds of torrents and systems of ruts they were raised universally to the condition and appearance of gravel walks in private parks.

The golden age of coaching began in the last ten years of the eighteenth century and lasted until about 1830. Regular timetables and a sustained average speed of 10 mph by the coaches of the Royal Mail meant that inter-city times were greatly reduced. The safe and elegant post coaches had names like *The Magnet, The Traveller* and *The Red Rover*. On the good, new roads ordinary stage coaches could manage about 4 or 5 mph, and even stage-waggons could maintain a steady 2 mph.

By the later years of the eighteenth century the terrors of travelling had been so reduced that people actually enjoyed making journeys; suddenly the country was filled with tourists. William Wordsworth (1770–1850) wrote so enthusiastically about the beauties of the English Lake District that his *Lyrical Ballads* (1798) caused the area to be swamped with nature pilgrims. He then complained about this invasion of visitors, which his poetry had brought to his doorstep. Similar complaints from residents of the Lake District have been increasing in volume every year since his death!

When the world's first iron bridge was opened over the River Severn in Shropshire in 1781, masses of sightseers flocked there. The present-day tourists who come in their millions to the little town of Ironbridge can buy copies of eighteenth-century prints showing these first trippers bowling over the deck of the bridge in their carriages and coaches, admiring the rugged sides of the gorge which it spans. The Wye Valley was also much visited and 'picturesque tours' became part of the education of the wealthy – travel had become fashionable.

The example set by British road-building techniques was swiftly followed, and road systems were improved all over Europe. All along these better roads, a great variety of well-sprung wheeled vehicles, including light coaches of superior design, hurtled at the gallop, pulled by relays of fresh horses. The travel industry was revitalised, and to complement these technical developments numbers of strategically placed post-houses, hotels and inns were built which offered safe and comfortable hospitality to travellers. This booming Dickensian period of road transport, which still inspires so many Christmas card scenes, was, however, destined to last for only 40 or 50 years.

The age of steam

The need for better roads had become more urgent because of the flowering of the Industrial Revolution. This was the most momentous period since the Renaissance; it was in fact a series of events brought about by the growth of scientific knowledge and its practical applications, which gave much greater control of the physical world and its resources than ever before. The use of new machinery driven by steam power and the large-scale smelting of iron by coal vastly increased the output of consumer goods. Iron engines were invented for steam coaches, iron wheels were manufactured, iron rails were laid, and finally came the logical outcome of combining all these elements – the first steam railway locomotive.

In 1804 an engine built by Richard Trevithick, a Cornishman, not only moved under its own power but also pulled five wagons and a passenger coach along a 10-mile stretch of tramway in South Wales. The age of the railway had arrived. A Scottish engineer, George Stephenson (1781–1848), built a railway between Liverpool and Manchester in 1830 which was the first exclusively to employ steam locomotives and offer regular goods and passenger services. This venture was so successful (it carried 445,000 passengers in its first year) that there was a series of private Acts of Parliament for the formation of railway companies and Britain was gripped by a fever of railway activity. By 1840 there were 1,860 miles of track; by 1855 8,000; and by 1870 more than 15,000.

One train could carry as many people as 30 stage coaches plus a large quantity of goods; there was no need for the surly coachman with his cry of 'No room on the coach!' – another carriage could simply be hooked on; passengers did not have to climb up over muddy wheels to sit exposed to all kinds of weather on top of a pile of luggage; and above all, there was the humanitarian aspect of not being dragged along by tired animals whipped on to keep to a schedule. Journeys were also much quicker, for example in 1750 London to Newcastle took six days by road; in 1850, by rail, it took nine and three-quarter hours. Similarly, in 1750 London to Bath took two days by road; in 1850, by rail, it took three and three-quarter hours.

By about the middle of the 1830s, this new and seemingly miraculous form of transport was putting an end to all the apparatus of coaching, coaching inns and turnpike roads. By 1841 the Royal Mail had been taken off the road and given to the railway.

Tourism can only ever be as good as travel technology allows it to be, and during this period transportation received a tremendous boost. For the first time in history people were no longer dependent on the power of their own muscles or the muscles of animals to get from place to place, nor did they have to rely on the variations of winds, tides and currents to cross seas and navigate rivers. Again there was an enormous increase in the spread of ideas and an expansion of business, just as there had been in the sixteenth century. The growth of the railway system in the 1840s meant that the less wealthy middle classes – themselves a product of the Industrial Revolution – could also travel considerable distances from home. Wales and Scotland began to emerge as tourist areas at about this time.

Since the early eighteenth century rich and aristocratic members of society had been in the habit of visiting spas for the good of their health, and for relaxation. Though some believed in the healing powers of mineral waters, places like Bath, Cheltenham, Buxton and Leamington had in fact always been towns visited for pleasure. The well-to-do had flocked there in their smart carriages to show off their clothes and manners to other fashionable visitors like themselves. This tradition persisted well into Victorian times and greater numbers began to take the waters, helped by the speedier travel of the railway age. Many of these places are visited by present-day tourists who come to admire their impressive Queen Anne and Regency townscapes, and most of them are still important cultural centres. In the last century, though, they were always elegant and exclusive. They were places where the mill-workers, steel-workers and miners of industrial areas would have been frowned upon.

By the 1850s the working classes that made up the bulk of the population of cities and industrial towns began to have more leisure time and money at their disposal. Wages rose and holidays lengthened, and in 1871 bank holidays, which were for everyone who worked, were established by law. The masses gladly took

British working classes at the seaside c. 1850

advantage of the accelerating revolution in steam-powered transport to visit the seaside for their first breaths of salt sea air.

Inhabitants of the grimy slums of London had always been able to use the Thames as a highway to escape from the suffocating city, but the coming of paddle steamers in the 1830s meant that river and coastal travel was cheaper, quicker and on a larger scale than ever before. The result was that Southend, Margate and Ramsgate became the Cockneys' playgrounds. Sailing from Liverpool and Birkenhead, paddle steamers began to open up the coast of North Wales by running holiday excursions to the developing seaside resorts of Llandudno, Colwyn Bay and Rhyl. Meanwhile from Blackpool and Morecambe, in the north of England, to Brighton and Folkestone in the south, from Scarborough and Yarmouth in the east, to Bournemouth and Torquay in the west, the coasts of Britain were invaded by trainloads of visitors clamouring for a sight of the sea and an abundance of noisy amusement.

This explosion of cheap travel for the working classes was partly the result of Gladstone's Railway Act of 1844 which established minimum standards for third-class passengers. Instead of open trucks with bare benches and boards, the railway companies had to provide a roof and proper seating. One train a day at least had to halt at every station for third-class passengers, and the maximum charge was to be one old penny (1d) per mile. Second-class carriages were more comfortable and were joined onto faster trains, but the wealthy travelled in sumptuous coaches that were first-class in every way: they were the state-of-the-art land transport of their time. Just as there were levels of transport to suit all classes, there had to be levels of accommodation to suit all pockets. At the top of the range, extravagant and ornate purpose-built hotels imitated the stately homes of the gentry they hoped to attract. Meals were served in huge dining-rooms and had many courses of costly dishes. The domestic routine of the hotels relied on great numbers of staff, who had been made to look and act as much as possible like servants in country houses. Architects echoed the same grandiose theme and built Victorian replicas of Tudor manors, Jacobean mansions, Gothic abbeys and French châteaux. The names of these establishments were meant to reflect the luxury which rich tourists might find within. Seaside towns which had started life as humble fishing-villages had their seafronts dominated by huge constructions with names like The Palace, The Majestic, The Splendide and The Grand.

Everyone wanted a bite of this new prosperity. Smaller, but still 'genteel' family hotels and guest-houses catered for second-class tourists, and until new rows of boarding houses could be completed to house the growing influx of visitors from lower social levels, humbler homes were hastily converted to offer spare bedrooms at modest prices. In some resorts there was a conflict of interests between sedate residents and ambitious tradespeople. Working-class customers brought great spending power to the seaside, but they also brought their undesirable local holiday traditions such as singing, shouting, dancing and drinking in the streets. Showmen and street entertainers followed the crowds and moved onto the piers and foreshores. In Blackpool the situation was resolved by a sort of social zoning. Residents and the 'better class of visitor' stuck to the safety of the North Shore which was at a distance from the station. The central area and the South Shore became the focus for rough and ready amusements. There were even two piers: the North Pier (1862), which offered sedate music and promenading, and the South Jetty (1868), noted for open-air dancing and cheap steamer trips. A study of the social origins of the different standards and types of travel, accommodation and entertainment quickly reveals the causes of the snobbery that for years has bedevilled the tourist industry.

By 1841 the railway had reached Leicester, and in that city there lived a 33-year-old Baptist lay preacher, who became the founding father of the modern tourist industry. Thomas Cook (1808–92) was a temperance campaigner who had started running cheap trips to keep the workers out of mischief and take their minds off drink. His first conducted tour, in 1841, was the 22-mile return trip from Leicester to Loughborough, and he organised a party of 570 people who travelled for a shilling each (5 new pence). This excursion was so successful that by 1845 he had opened the great travel business which, though now internationally owned, still bears his name.

Britain had gained a head start in the Industrial Revolution, partly because the necessary raw materials lay beneath our soil but also because many of the early scientists and engineers happened to be born in this country at the right point in history. Within less than 10 years, however, the rest of the world had caught up. By the time of the Great Exhibition of 1851, which was meant to show Britain's pride in its advanced manufacturing skills, foreign competitors had developed their own industries and came to compare rather than to envy. Nevertheless, during 1851, more foreign visitors entered Britain than ever before to wonder at Paxton's marvellous Crystal Palace, set in the middle of Hyde Park. It was probably the first purpose-built exhibition hall, and the whole event was so successful that it sparked off a series of international trade fairs and exhibitions that are still the biggest generators of business tourism today.

Right from the beginning of the 1800s a pattern of touring had been established on the Continent. Spas and *kursaals*, casinos and

Paxton's marvellous Crystal Palace (1851)

horse-racing courses had sprung up all over Europe in the comparative peace that followed the Napoleonic Wars. Seaside resorts also began to flourish around the coasts of France, Belgium, Germany, Holland and Italy. These varied in detail according to their location and climate, but their general character became remarkably similar and they developed at about the same rate. Resorts on more northerly coasts followed the British example very closely with sea bathing, a promenade, a pier plus a variety of entertainments and accommodation.

As noted above, the construction of better roads made it easier for fashionable tourism to speed waves of wealthy international pleasure-seekers and adventurers all around Europe. By the middle of the nineteenth century, though, the pace at which the world was becoming smaller was much more rapid. The railway lines which spanned continents carried trains that had sleeping, dining, club and observation cars. The vast distances of nineteenth-century America were opened up by powerful railway engines which could pull dozens of carriages through difficult country for days on end. Coal-fired iron passenger ships like Brunel's *Great Britain* (1843) and *Great Eastern* (1858) were designed to carry up to 4,000 passengers. Previously, wooden sailing vessels, which were dangerous and relied on unpredictable wind-power, could accommodate only 200 passengers at the most. Some steamships, following ocean routes which had encircled the globe, developed into the floating luxury hotels that were known as liners. The 60 great ships of the P & O line regularly took thousands of men, women and children to and from the Far East, both for pleasure and for purposes of trade and administration. Cunard, on the other hand, were advertising 'Steam to New York' as early as 1860. By the late nineteenth century, they dominated the transatlantic routes so thoroughly that they had ships leaving every day on rapid journeys to and from America. In 1907 their famous luxury liner, the *Mauretania*, powered by the new steam turbines invented by Charles Parsons, won the Blue Riband for the fastest crossing from Britain to the USA. Tourists were moving around by the million, actually enjoying their travel and going ever farther and faster in the quest for new horizons.

The motor car

Between 1885 and 1886, while British engineers were still busily occupied with the ultimate development of steam power, two German inventors, Gottlieb Daimler and Carl Benz, independently devised the first motor cars with petrol-driven internal combustion engines. During the 1890s and almost until the beginning of the First World War, the motor car was a very expensive, rather uncomfortable and somewhat unreliable means of transport. This situation was changed dramatically in 1914 when Henry Ford introduced the technique of mass-producing easy-to-drive, dependable cars. 'I will build a car for the great multitude', he declared, and the multitude eagerly accepted his offer. Two world wars speeded up the development of internal combustion engineering and led to the creation of the modern car as we know it. One result of the growth in car ownership in the early twentieth century was the revival of road travel. The middle classes began to use the independence of the family car to explore secluded rural corners, and there was a new interest in old towns and villages. Coaching inns had slumbered and fallen into disrepair for almost a century since losing their trade to the railway hotels. The re-opening of the old highways and byways, however, brought a trickle of travellers, which by the 1920s had become such a considerable flow that traditional post-houses had to extend and refurbish their facilities. The loose road surfaces which could turn to mud and dust were coated and bound with smooth asphalt. Long-disused stables were turned into garages, as grooms and ostlers became mechanics and chauffeurs. The coming of mass-motoring in the 1920s and '30s led to the building of guest- and road-houses alongside the new arterial roads which cut direct lines across the countryside and the bypasses that looped around towns.

Charabancs, and later motor coaches, catered for those who could not afford cars of their own, and coach tours inclusive of accommodation and fare became popular by the 1920s. Cyclists and motorcyclists added to the flood of travellers seeking the joys of the open road, and many cottages hung out the 'wheeled wing', the sign of the Cyclists' Touring Club. Undergraduates, intellectuals and writers wandered around on foot and bicycle, encouraged by the chain of hostels opened up by the Youth Hostel Association to cater for inexpensive holidays in the countryside. Moors and mountains, castles and cathedrals became the object of tourist interest as well as seaside resorts and spas.

All this new activity on old roads which had been designed centuries before motorised traffic was ever thought of led to congestion, delays in travel and a great increase in road accidents. Britain lagged behind in road-building for decades compared to other European countries. France had long and straight well-surfaced roads, which greatly aided the development of their motor and tourist industry; by 1935 Germany had built its excellent system of *Autobahns*; and Italy soon followed with efficient *autostradas* that speeded trade and tourism. There were recommendations for a national network of motorways in Britain in the mid-1930s, but because of the Second World War practical proposals did not appear until 1946, and in fact it was 1958 before Britain's first stretch of motorway (the Preston Bypass) was opened. This was as welcome as it was overdue because between the years 1952 and 1962 expenditure on cars and motor cycles had increased by 600 per cent.

Air-travel

Throughout history wars have caused disruption and damage to normal international life. One of the less harmful side-effects, though, is that war often leads to a leap forward in travel technology, and that is just what happened in 1919. The first commercial air services depended heavily upon the flying experience gained by pilots in the First World War, and the first civil passenger planes were converted warplanes. Britain can claim the honour of having started the first international passenger air services: soon after midday on 25 August 1919, a four-seat conversion of the De Havilland DH 9A day-bomber took off from Hounslow airfield to carry two passengers to Paris. On the same day a civil version of the Handley Page 0/400 heavy bomber left Cricklewood to take 11 passengers to the same destination. International commercial aviation had begun in a spirit of healthy competition!

Throughout the interwar years Croydon was the chief British airport, and handled a reasonable amount of international traffic against stiff competition from the French airlines. At this time Britain, along with several other European countries, still had an extensive empire, and in 1924 the British government created Imperial Airways as a subsidised monopoly. This service concentrated on long-distance overseas routes, and by 1931 passengers could travel from Southampton on the great Kent-class flying boats built by Short Brothers. These were comfortable, four-engined sixteen-seaters, in which passengers reclined on luxurious seats and ate gourmet meals, prepared in the aircraft's galley by master chefs.

Flights to Europe had been rather neglected in the inter-war years, so in 1946 British European Airways was formed to compete with the national airlines of other countries. Longer flights, such as the routes to Australia, were served by the British Overseas Airways Corporation (BOAC), but these two state companies were merged in 1972 as British Airways (BA). Social and geographical mobility increased after the Second World War, and, stimulated by the six war years of development in aircraft technology, the network of national and international flights spread rapidly. Flying, however, was not for everyone who wished to take a holiday, as air fares remained prohibitively expensive for years.

Travelling abroad on holiday was itself quite a rarity for British people. It is amazing to discover that the following passage from *The Sunday Times Book of Britain* was written as late as 1961: its snobbery and condescension seem to belong to an earlier age.

> Foreign travel, once largely confined to middle and upper income groups, is now enjoyed by wage earners too. More than 3 million Britons now go abroad annually on holiday, compared with 1,200,000 in 1947.
>
> Many go no further than Ireland or the Channel Islands, but two thirds visit the Continent and the rest of the world, and a large number of the new travellers are working-class people. A wry joke among middle-class housewives is that they must take their holidays at Britain's dreary seaside resorts, while their servants – if they still have servants – go to France and Switzerland.

The real breakthrough into the mass market for foreign holidays came in 1950 when Vladimir Reitz of Horizon Travel, London organised the first package tour by air. By booking all the seats in a 32-seater aircraft, he was said to have chartered it; the unit cost of seats on the full aircraft was then much lower than the scheduled airlines could offer. By combining these cheap air tickets with travel from the airport to block-booked, full-board accommodation in Corsica, and charging an all-inclusive price, Reitz had invented the inclusive tour by charter (ITC).

Numbers of passengers on international flights from Britain grew enormously during the post-war years, especially in the 1960s and '70s. In 1939 there were 170,000 passengers, in 1970 21 million and in 1980 41 million. Britain could also take the credit for having begun the jet age for airline traffic when, in 1952, the De Havilland Comet made the first British commercial jet flight from London to Johannesburg. Comet, operated by BOAC, was also the first jet airliner to fly on the North Atlantic route. This initiative was soon lost to the major American aircraft builders such as Boeing and Douglas, whose faster, higher-capacity jetliners cut flight times substantially and increased public confidence in aviation. These aircraft were the greatest single factor in increasing the scale of the modern tourist industry.

One rather sad effect of this increase in cheaper and faster flights was the gradual disappearance of the great ocean liners. By the end of the 1950s shipping lines all around the world realised that their passenger services could not possibly compete with air travel. Some companies closed down altogether and others, such as Cunard and P & O, adapted their ships and their thinking to the growing demand for leisurely cruising holidays. These two businesses, along with several other international competitors, have had great success in this new sphere, and it is still possible to travel the waters of the world in luxury and style.

Meanwhile, back in the air, competition to state airlines from independent private companies increased in the 1960s, and fares became even cheaper. In 1977, with the introduction of Laker Airways' 'walk-on' transatlantic service, there began a price-cutting war which continues to this day. The activities of entrepreneurs like Richard Branson, chairman of Virgin Atlantic Airways, have created another travel revolution by bringing long-haul holidays within the reach of millions. The impact of the reductions can be judged by the fact that in 1992 a Virgin Atlantic one-way ticket from London to New York cost £99. At the same time, the price of BA's one-way shuttle flight from London to Glasgow or Edinburgh was £103. BA still carries the flag for Britain as a national airline, but since its privatisation in 1987 it has traded as British Airways Plc and has no government subsidy. BA performs remarkably well against other national airlines which compete fiercely for the busy transatlantic routes, and is not badly threatened by charter flights since its main profit comes from business and first-class travellers.

The boom in cheap package tours to Mediterranean sunspots and inexpensive holidays in exotic destinations ended the heyday of our native seaside with all its joys and all its drawbacks. There are, however, signs of a revival in the fortunes of British seaside resorts. Congested airports, together with falling standards of hospitality at many venues along the overcrowded Mediterranean coastlines, have made families look nearer to home for short breaks and annual holidays. Visitors from Europe, Japan and America too are flocking in increasing numbers to sample the charm and atmosphere of Britain since our tourism industry has started to give a better-quality service and improve its image.

Internationally, the desire to visit unknown places shows no sign of abating. Amazement at the novelties of travel and delight at discovering our common humanity are everywhere replacing the fear and hostility towards all things foreign that characterised travel as recently as 50 years ago. There are encouraging indications too that the era of uncontrolled exploitation of the resources and peoples of the globe is ending. The realisation that the planet as a whole is our home, and that everyone is responsible for it, is the ultimate beneficial result of increased tourism. These developments will be discussed further in Chapter 5.

Assignment: Safe suntans

In recent years doctors, scientists and politicians in Britain, America and Australia have become concerned about the destruction of the ozone layer, that screens the Earth from the sun's harmful ultraviolet rays. Without the protection of that layer there is an increased risk of skin damage and even skin cancer unless proper precautions are taken when exposed to sunlight. This is a growing concern now that greater numbers of people than ever before are taking more holidays in hot countries. Study the following selection of facts and opinions:

1 Excessive ultraviolet radiation from the sun that should be blocked by the layer of ozone in the upper atmosphere is reaching the ground.
2 The ozone shield is being destroyed by pollution. Chlorine gases used in refrigeration and air-conditioning equipment are eating up the protective ozone layer.
3 The sunrays which cause tanning contain bands of ultra-violet radiation (UV). The two main wavebands are: UVA and UVB. Both of these can damage the skin. Their intensity is greatest between 11am and 3pm.
4 i) UVA radiation goes deeply into the skin and tends to make it dry, leathery and prematurely wrinkled.
ii) UVB radiation is soaked up by the surface of the skin and stimulates the production of the tanning pigment, melanin. UVB causes sunburn and is considered by many experts to be responsible for most skin cancers.

5 In Britain there has been a 40 per cent increase in skin cancer between 1979 and 1991. There are now 28,000 cases a year and the total is rising. Skin cancer is the second most common cancer in the UK.

6 There are two types of skin cancer caused by the sun:

i) *Malignant melanoma*. This is fairly rare but is extremely dangerous. In 1993 Dr Julia Newton, consultant dermatologist with the Imperial Cancer Research Fund's skin tumour laboratory in London, warned that the incidence of malignant melanoma doubles every ten years. She said it has one of the fastest rates of increase of all cancers in the UK, with about 3,600 new cases every year. That represents a rise of more than 100 per cent since 1974. It causes 1,200 deaths every year and is almost twice as common in women as in men. It affects younger people as well as older people of both sexes.

Melanomas pose most threat to people who are sun-sensitive. They are especially at risk if they spend most of their life indoors in temperate regions but then take a two-week holiday in a hot, sunny place.

ii) *Non-melanoma*. This is much more common than melanoma. It is, however, less dangerous and can, in most cases, be cured. There are approximately 30,000 new cases every year, and the number of new cases has increased by almost 50 per cent since 1974. It causes about 500 deaths every year and it affects men and women equally. It is commonly found in the 55 plus age group.

Some authorities connect non-melanomas to long-term exposure to sunlight. Outdoor workers (e.g. foresters, farmers, construction workers, professional sportspeople, etc.) are especially at risk.

7 *Symptoms*. Most people have moles and/or freckles. Such things are normally harmless but any that grow, itch, bleed or, indeed, alter in any noticeable way should receive medical attention.

8 *Skin types*. Some people are able to acquire a rich tan quickly and with no ill effects. They have a naturally high sun protection factor (SPF). It is worth remembering, though, that *anyone* can burn after continued exposure if the sun is hot enough. Generally speaking, fair-skinned, fair-haired people with light-coloured eyes do burn more easily and are more at risk from melanoma than those with darker skin, hair and eyes. People who burn easily are said to be more sun-sensitive. Babies and young children are always at risk from sunburn and excessive heat.

9 *Types of climate*. The danger of sunburn is obviously greater in very sunny climates. Sunlight is much more intense in Mediterranean regions, the tropics, the semi-tropics and the antipodes than it is in the northern hemisphere.

People who take 'winter sun' holidays can be particularly at risk. This is also relevant to those who take skiing breaks as well as water-sport and beach holidays. Sunlight is intensified when reflected by snow or water. It is possible to burn whilst swimming, or, by reflection, when in light shade.

10 *Protection*. Research work by Dr Robin Marks and his colleagues from the University of Melbourne has provided evidence that the proper use of strong sunscreen creams can help both to prevent skin cancers and reverse potential damage caused by sunburn. The use of sensible, protective clothing and hats can also remove much of the danger. Sunfilter creams and lotions absorb the harmful sunrays and prevent skin damage. The active element in modern preparations is generally PABA (Para Amino Benzoic Acid), which occurs naturally in the body and is also known as Vitamin H. Such creams also have moisturising compounds in them to protect the elasticity of the skin. Protective preparations have SPFs which range from a low 4–2 to a high 25–20.

The areas of the body which burn most badly are the face, the ears and the neck. Any area where the skin is thinly stretched over the bone (e.g. shins, scalp, etc.) is particularly vulnerable.

It is essential to tan gradually, even when using protective creams. Usually it takes three or four days for the tanning pigment to develop.

Working in groups and using the information above to help you, conduct some further research[1] into the dangers of sunburn, and:

a) organise and mount an exhibition which could be displayed in the foyer of schools, colleges, community centres, etc. to warn of the dangers of skin damage on holiday
b) prepare a 15-minute talk to accompany the exhibition
c) adapt your information to write a useful and readable illustrated article which could be included in an in-flight magazine for both scheduled and charter flights.

Remember that your task is to warn, inform and reassure. Take care not to alarm or frighten off clients who might be encountering these facts for the first time.

[1] You will need to look at some of the sun protective preparations currently on sale and read the literature which accompanies them. In order to help you assess their degree of usefulness, write to the manufacturers for further information. You might also find it helpful to write to the:
Health Education Authority, Hamilton House, Mabledon Place, London WC1H 9TX

3 Who makes it possible?

Right from the beginning tourism has been made possible only through the efforts of those who are willing and able to provide transport, accommodation and food for travellers. As late as the end of the nineteenth century and the first half of the twentieth century, provision for tourism was left to the working of market forces. Whenever there was a necessity to get from one place to another, some enterprising character or other would charge a sum of money for making it possible. If the demand arose for food and shelter for travellers, there would be an entrepreneur to seize the opportunity and set up in business to meet it. Ports, railway stations, roads, inns, hotels and restaurants were all built and situated where and when they were needed.

Reasons for intervention by governments

This situation would still hold good today, if the industry had not become much more complex in a more crowded world. Mass tourism can bring massive problems. Competition for customers has intensified, and the traditional objectives of moving, accommodating and feeding tourists have been supplemented by a greater necessity for attracting and entertaining them.

When a country becomes integrated into the international tourist network, there follows an inevitable involvement with hotel chains, national airlines, international credit-card companies and tour operators. This can lead to other difficulties. Publicity campaigns must be pitched at the right level to attract the optimum number of the sort of visitors that the country, the region or the resort wishes to cater for in terms of spending power, social behaviour and type of attraction demanded. Commercial operators often market and promote venues haphazardly in the name of growth and expansion, but governments have recently taken a hard look at the heedless world of the developer. As a result they have come to realise that they must exercise their functions of planning, management and control if their tourist industries are to remain viable.

New causes for concern

Governments have always had to take some interest in the numbers of visitors entering into, staying in, or passing through their countries. Genuine tourists have usually been received as guests, but national authorities have had to be on their guard against undesirable elements such as political or religious extremists, international criminals and terrorists. Nowadays controls and checks are often imposed to combat the dangers of drug trafficking, illegal immigration and the spread of disease. Since tourism has become such a huge, diverse and fragmented industry central authorities have accepted national responsibility for the security and welfare of tourists in a way that individual enterprises could not contemplate. When enormous numbers of people are being moved around the globe by land, sea and air the problems of control and safety become so big that international cooperation and agreement are needed to solve them.

Impact on destinations

Until comparatively recently it had not been realised that the sheer volume of visitors arriving at any popular destination would make lasting changes to the lives and environment of the people already living there. When great numbers of extra people come to inhabit an area for a holiday season, they increase the demands made on the infrastructure of that area. (The word 'infrastructure' here refers to facilities such as roads, railways, airport runways, deep water docks for large ships, and provision for the parking and circulation of road traffic at terminals. It also includes utilities and services such as supplies of water, electricity, gas, drainage, sewage and rubbish disposal). Only when the infrastructure is in place can a responsible government allow the building of the superstructure. ('Superstructure', in terms of tourism, means buildings at airports and ports, hotels and other forms of accommodation provision, food outlets, shops, attractions and sites of interest.)

Governments now realise that there has to be a correlation between the numbers of visitors entering their countries and the limitations of their national resources and facilities. There is a growing feeling that special regard should be paid to the needs of the host population when considering extending the infrastructure or the superstructure – there are social and cultural issues to be considered as well as economic ones. After all, the permanent residents of a country or area are the ones who should have first claim on the use of space, water supplies and the distribution of food. Their traditional way of life has to be safeguarded; there must be a balance of fairness between nationals and visitors.

Positive advantages

On the other hand, tourism usually creates wealth for the host country by stimulating economic growth. The foreign currency which it brings in establishes a sound balance of payments situation. The result is that governments have themselves traditionally encouraged tourism as much as is possible without depriving their own populations or offering an inferior service to tourists. Some fortunate countries have got the balance right and have become very prosperous through tourism. They proudly exhibit their heritage and culture along with their natural geographical advantages in such a way that both visitors and hosts are satisfied. They manage natural resources skilfully, and when infrastructures and superstructures are improved and extended to serve the needs of tourists they are also designed to be of lasting benefit to the country's inhabitants.

Expo '92

The best example of good tourism practice during the 1990s was seen in Spain. Expo '92 was a great universal exhibition in Seville,

Expo '92

which ran for six months from April 1992. It was sited on La Cartuja Island across the River Guadalquivir from the ancient Andalusian city. It opened up an underdeveloped region; it attracted millions of visitors, generating much business and bringing in hard currency; it served as a showplace for the best in international architecture and technology; and it served to demonstrate the power of European cooperation.

More importantly, the exhibition took a look at the lessons of history and attempted to explore the future of the world. Cartuja '93 was established, a body which will produce studies on and alternatives for the future. And when Expo '92 ended it left behind, as a permanent memorial to its aims, a legacy of new roads, bridges, public buildings and gardens for the use and enjoyment of the people of Seville.

It might be useful to summarise briefly how and why governments have become so deeply involved in modern tourism:

Opportunities

- the possibility of earning foreign currency and improving balance of payments
- gaining increased tax revenue from Value Added Tax (VAT), import duties, motorway tolls, airport dues and fees at ports
- attracting foreign capital for the improvement of infrastructure and superstructure
- levies on tourist accommodation
- creating employment from jobs in tourism, and so gaining from income tax and reduced benefit payments
- increasing economic activity by residents in tourist areas
- incentives to revitalise neglected areas and attractions
- stimulating interest in galleries, museums, theatres, national monuments, etc.
- the political advantages of projecting a good image of one's own country
- the political advantages of establishing friendly ties with other countries.

Responsibilities

- to lead and coordinate tourism
- to give help in promoting tourism at home and abroad
- to provide financial assistance to agencies and tourist boards

- to develop a national planning strategy for tourism
- to make investment decisions and participate in marketing strategies
- to oversee and approve proposals made by the private sector
- to guarantee the safety and comfort of tourists
- to maintain or improve the quality of the tourist experience and facilitate visitor flows
- to preserve and improve the quality of the built and natural environment and avoid damaging the ecology
- to coordinate and improve the education and training of all those who work in the industry.

National tourist organisations

For the reasons mentioned above, most countries have now established national tourist organisations (NTOs) in an attempt to make their tourist industries work to the best advantage of all concerned.

NTOs vary in type and structure from one country to another. Generally speaking, countries which have a well-established tourist industry (such as Austria and the USA) have a system of devolving influence and responsibility from the centre of government to the regions and localities of the country. Some countries have a sort of ready-made structure for regional tourist organisation: America, for example, has its constituent states, which already have a considerable degree of self-government and are large areas each with a separate identity. Germany too is a federation, so that Bavaria and Saxony, for instance, form natural units for the management of tourism. Switzerland has its cantons which act as regional centres. The United Kingdom (which will be looked at in detail later in the chapter) may be separated into England, Scotland, Wales and Northern Ireland, at national levels, and then subdivided into regions. It is halfway between a federal and a centralised system.

Countries where tourism is fairly new or is being revived (such as Nicaragua and Cuba) tend to have very centralised NTOs with close state control over every kind of tourist activity. The need for central control and a firm tourism policy is especially important in countries which are just embarking on promoting tourism after years of isolation. They have observed that gross overdevelopment occurs when areas of unspoiled natural beauty create high tourist demand. The situation becomes worse when capital is made available at reasonable rates, and there is a plentiful supply of cheap labour from economically deprived local populations. This happened in the 1960s and '70s on Spain's 'concrete costas', and the ensuing hyperdevelopment has eventually led to the destruction of picturesque areas and falling visitor numbers. Spain's neighbour, Portugal, is concerned that a similar situation should not unbalance the pattern of development along its shores. The centralised National Tourist Office there is seeking to open up neglected districts in the interior of the country. It has also combined with Air Portugal (the state airline) to raise awareness of national identity by running a 'Discover the real Algarve' campaign.

There may be other reasons for centralisation too. The Netherlands, for example, has a highly centralised NTO, because control over visitor flow and provision of facilities is most important in a small, densely populated nation. Even within the United Kingdom there are exceptions which stand outside the hierarchy of the NTO: the Isle of Man, the Channel Islands and Northern Ireland have their own statutory bodies which exist independently. It is fair then to say that, though they may be similar, no two NTOs are exactly alike. This is because they have developed in response to the situations existing in their own countries and the demands made upon them by the modern pressures of tourism.

The world perspective

As was noted earlier, no single country can develop a tourist policy or run an efficient tourist industry on its own: cooperation with other nations is essential. Just imagine, for instance, trying to construct a flight-plan from the UK to Indonesia or Australia without a knowledge of international air-space regulations. How could any travel agency in, say, the USA organise worry-free group holidays to a Central African country such as Zambia without consultation about the health risks that might arise? Think how vital it is when visiting a sub-continent like India, where religion is of great national importance, to be aware of possible problems which could be caused by ignorance. Could any sophisticated, industrialised country be allowed nowadays to exploit the people and ruin the beautiful landscapes of an underdeveloped country without attracting some criticism from other nations?

For these – and many other reasons arising from the multi-faceted nature of tourism – it is clear that anyone who thinks in terms of one country or one region does not understand the realities of the industry.

The World Tourism Organisation

- one in every 15 of the world's workforce and one in every 10 of Europe's workforce are employed in travel and tourism
- Europe is the world's leading tourist centre; it attracts 60 per cent of all international arrivals, compared with 19 per cent to the Americas and 11 per cent to East Asia
- the world spends three times as much on tourism as on defence
- world travel and tourism is growing almost twice as fast as the world's gross national product (GNP).

(Source: Address to Chartered Institute of Marketing, March 1993, by Alan Jefferson, international marketing director for the BTA.)

The above facts illustrate why, to coordinate the efforts of NTOs, the World Tourism Organisation (WTO) was founded. This is a unique partnership of differing interests which has the promotion of sustainable tourism throughout the world as its main aim. It is an international tourism-linking organisation; a producer of statistics on tourism movements and development; a promoter of tourism and its contribution to economic development, international understanding, peace and prosperity; and a research body which sponsors regional seminars and workshops, technical cooperation programmes and vocational training. The WTO has committees on environment, facilitation, and security and protection.

Sometimes the lack of positive international action can be rather disappointing to committed ecologists. It is often difficult to reach world-wide agreement on such matters as forest and coastline conservation. Unfortunately, there are still a few nations which pay very little regard to the need for interaction between tourism, the environment and development. Nevertheless, the WTO is there to highlight some of the challenges facing tourism providers in the 1990s and its formation has been a tremendous step in the right direction.

The private and support sectors

In spite of what has been noted about the need for interest and help from NTOs and local government authorities, the fact remains that the world's tourist industry consists mainly of thousands of businesses in the private/commercial sector. Even though public and private bodies are closely intertwined, the private sector is the real driving force in tourism, as well as being the major employer. Some of these businesses are great multinationals like Club Med,

Butlins, Thomas Cook, Airtours, American Express, Lunn Poly, Novotel, Hilton, Holiday Inn, Disney, Delta Air Lines, P & O Cruises, and Avis Rent-A-Car to name but a few familiar market leaders. The surprising fact is that the top 100 companies probably account for less than one-third of tourist spending. The great majority of private tourist enterprises are part of a vast spectrum of small- and medium-sized businesses, some of which only employ one or two people.

Free enterprise in the western world is a creative force in society and there has to be an emphasis on commercial realism in the tourism industry. Nevertheless, someone also has to exercise a sense of responsibility, question the decisions of policy-forming bodies, monitor standards and advise on forward planning. Entrepreneurs can become too enthusiastic. Government agencies can become remote and bureaucratic. As a result, there has emerged a world-wide network of advisory, voluntary and charitable bodies which help to solve the problems which arise from the growth of tourism. Some of these bodies fall into the 'government' sector, some belong to the 'private' sector and others work with both sectors. The membership of such bodies comprises academics, educationalists, experienced practitioners and representatives of interested parties. It includes both professionals and informed amateurs, 'watchdogs' and promoters. Of the people who make up these groups, some are paid employees and others are honorary officials who give their time freely. The main concern of all is that tourism should always have the best aims, and should not harm, disappoint or neglect anyone who comes into contact with it.

There are many examples of help given to tourism by such organisations, but there is only enough space here to mention four British voluntary bodies. The rising international interest in promoting and facilitating holidays and travel for disabled and deprived people makes these instances especially worth noting because similar ideas are being implemented in other countries.

Help given by voluntary bodies in the UK

The National Trust, the world's largest conservation charity, publishes a useful free booklet *Information for Visitors with Disabilities*, which details facilities at the Trust's properties in England, Wales and Northern Ireland. In addition, the Trust has raised money and secured sponsorship from private trade and industry to provide powered, self-drive one- and two-seater buggies which are available at many of their parks and gardens. These vehicles not only enhance visits for people with impaired mobility, but also allow their companions to enjoy their visits more.

The Royal National Institute for the Blind (RNIB) has developed Register Enforced Automated Control Technique (REACT), a revolutionary mobility guide. Each visually impaired visitor is given a REACT card, which sets off recorded messages of welcome and gives directions to and descriptions of exhibits, attractions and so on. Flambards Theme Park in Helston, Cornwall was the first to use the system, in 1990, but many galleries, museums and heritage centres are also adopting it.

The Family Holiday Association (FHA) is a most valuable national charity, which helps people who have not had a holiday for years, if ever. It makes grants to underprivileged families who live in squalid housing conditions because of poverty, unemployment, ill-health or disability. The FHA relies entirely on donations and the help of volunteer workers.

Other tourism suppliers are also coming to realise that there is a need to open up new holiday possibilities to the disabled, rather than exclude them by default. Those who plan and build hotels, leisure facilities, catering outlets and so on are now listening carefully to the representatives of organisations that represent the disadvantaged. The premier body supplying information and support for disabled and disadvantaged people is the Holiday Care Service (HCS). They produce the *Accessible Accommodation Guide* – 14 guides, in fact, which cover the whole of the UK. The guides are produced in large print to assist those with partial sight and visual impairment, and in addition to lists of accommodation contain details of accessible attractions, 'shopmobility' schemes and area access information.

When one considers that there are 6.7 million people in the UK with disabilities and that one in four families is affected by disablement, it becomes obvious that all organisations who help the physically disabled, the mentally handicapped and the visually impaired are providing for a large sector of the tourism market. More than 200 hotels are in the scheme, and as well as offering discounted rates they are inspected by the HCS to confirm the assurance that their accommodation will be accessible.

The British system

To make the relationship between the private and support sectors more clear, it will be helpful to take a closer look at the British tourist industry. The following is a summary of the country's tourism structure, which has proved, generally speaking, a very successful system – so successful, in fact, that elements of it have been adopted by many other countries.

1 The *wholly involved* sector (whether government or private, which deals mainly with staying and day visitors):

- statutory and other tourist boards
- accommodation
- tour operators
- travel agencies and other travel organisers
- commercial attractions.

2 The *partially involved* sector (facilities and services only partially used by tourists and day visitors, but also used by locals and other individuals following their everyday business):

- ministries, statutory bodies and other agencies whose work touches upon those activities which make up tourism (e.g. employment, environment, transport, agriculture, aviation, etc.)
- retail and catering outlets
- transport operators (air, sea, road and rail)
- leisure centres and country parks
- museums and galleries
- arts and entertainment
- sporting organisations.

3 Other bodies which advise on, help and regulate tourism can, as we have noted, have as their base an official, commercial or voluntary organisation. For example:

- education and training establishments (e.g. ABTA National Training Board, the Hotel and Catering Training Company (HCTC), the Institute of Linguists, tourism and leisure departments of universities and colleges, etc.)
- market-research organisations and consultancies (e.g. the British Tourist Authority and English Tourist Board (BTA/ETB) Marketing Division reports and surveys, UK Tourism Survey (UKTS), the Henley Centre for Forecasting, the European Travel Commission (ETC), Mintel, Phillips and Drew, Ventures Consultancy, Horwath International, Travel and Tourism Research, Ltd., Matrix Corporate Affairs Consultants, etc.)
- professional and trade associations (e.g. the Tourism Society, the Institute of Travel and Tourism, the International Association of Tour Managers, ABTA, the Institute of Directors, the British Association of Tourism Officers (BATO), the Chief Leisure Officers' Association,

the Museums Association, chambers of commerce, training and enterprise councils (TEC), etc.)
- the media and telecommunications (e.g. the Guild of Travel Writers, the Guild of Guide Lecturers, etc.)
- academic and scientific associations (e.g. Centre des Hautes Etudes Touristiques, the Centre for Environmental Interpretation, the International Association of Scientific Experts)
- certain voluntary and charitable bodies (e.g. the National Trust, the Civic Trust, the Ramblers' Association, the Tidy Britain Group, the Council for the Preservation of Rural England (CPRE), the Family Holiday Association, the Holiday Care Service, the Royal National Institute for the Blind (RNIB), Age Concern, Physically Handicapped and Able-Bodied (PHAB).

Britain has a three-tier organisational structure: national level; regional level; and local level.

National level

At national level there are central government ministries and departments which are concerned with leisure, recreation and tourism. The heads of these bodies are cabinet ministers who have a powerful voice in the running of the country. The ones most relevant to our studies are: the Department of National Heritage; the Department of the Environment; the Department of Trade and Industry; the Ministry of Agriculture, Fisheries and Food; the Ministry of Transport; the Department of Education and Science; the Ministry of Civil Aviation; the Department of Health; the Department of Employment; the Welsh Office; and the Scottish Office.

In order to help ministries with the complex, detailed work of administration, planning, finance and promotion, Parliament has passed laws to establish agencies and other statutory bodies. They are called 'statutory bodies' because their authority comes from statutes – Acts of Parliament, written laws and Royal Charters.

The Act of Parliament which set up the British Tourist Authority (BTA), the English Tourist Board (ETB), the Scottish Tourist Board (STB) and the Welsh Tourist Board (WTB) was the Development of Tourism Act, 1969. Northern Ireland already had its own tourist board (NITB) established under separate legislation (the Development of Tourist Traffic Act, 1948). Before it became an official body the BTA was a voluntary association of commercial organisations that was started in the 1930s with the aim of encouraging people from overseas to visit Britain. In 1969 it gained a proper administrative structure to carry on that important work in conjunction with the other UK tourist boards. Since 1969 the BTA has been funded by grants from central government, which in turn draws its financing from tax revenue.

The objectives of the BTA

BTA 🇬🇧
British Tourist Authority

1 To maximise the benefit to the economy of tourism to Britain from abroad while working world-wide in partnership with the private and public sector organisations involved in the industry and the ETB, STB and WTB.

2 To identify the requirements of visitors to Britain, whatever their origin, and to stimulate the improvement of the quality of product and the use of technology to meet them.

3 To spread the economic benefits of tourism to Britain more widely and particularly to areas with tourism potential and higher than average levels of unemployment.

4 To encourage tourism to Britain in off-peak periods.

5 To ensure that the Authority makes the most cost-effective use of resources in pursuing its objectives

6 To meet these objectives in close cooperation with the national and regional tourist boards, local authorities and other tourism interests by:

- collaborating with the industry and other interests to promote Great Britain as a tourist destination and encourage support for the BTA's cooperative marketing strategies
- consulting with the industry and overseas sources to determine the requirements of visitors to Britain
- researching the requirements of different overseas markets and segments to advise on product development and marketing opportunities; evaluating trends in the industry and their implications for visitor requirements
- encouraging the development and promotion of attractions and facilities attractive to visitors to Britain, and in particular those available in areas of higher than average unemployment and in off-peak periods
- setting clear objectives for the Authority's own marketing activities and measuring the results against these objectives
- preparing and keeping an up-to-date strategy for the

development and promotion of tourism from overseas
- enhancing the status of tourism as an attractive sector for
employment by stimulating education and training.

(Source: *BTA Policy Statement*, 1993.)

The BTA works in close collaboration with the National Tourist
Boards of Scotland and Wales and the 12 English Regional Tourist
Boards to coordinate a strong national/regional participation in
promotional activities overseas. Each tourist board produces an
overseas marketing plan in conjunction with the BTA, that takes
account of regional and national product strengths and matches
these with appropriate overseas markets. The resulting series of
initiatives is offered to local authorities and commercial companies
as an ideal opportunity to co-participate in a range of targeted promotions. These joint exercises offer:

- potentially reduced costs on a shared basis
- greater impact
- increased joint investment
- a range of well-targeted promotions in relevant markets
- the ability to be represented in a greater number of
markets than individually.

The BTA gives help to other tourist boards by advising about and
participation in:

- consumer exhibitions
- direct mail to repeat visitors
- regional/national guides distributed overseas
- travel trade events
- sales missions
- journalism/travel trade visits.

The funding and status of the BTA/ETB

The Department of National Heritage is responsible for allocating cash to the BTA/ETB. In
1993–94 the aid granted was £32 million, and in
addition to this the BTA raised more than £17
million from non-governmental partners. Some head-office functions such as finance, personnel, policy and information are shared
by the BTA and ETB, which are both located at Thames Tower,
Hammersmith, London.

Any government spending squeeze (due to recession or a policy to
keep down burdens on the taxpayer) can mean job cuts in the agencies and the limitation of activities such as promotions, preserva-

tion of the heritage and systems of hotel grading. In February 1993 such reductions in funding led to the BTA shedding 28 jobs in all areas of activity and at all levels. At the same time the ETB lost 43 of its 139 posts from the London headquarters. Between the years 1993 and 1996 the ETB are facing a grant cut of about 40 per cent; a drop from £15.6 million to £9.1 million.

Both the BTA and the ETB have complained that tourism is regarded by central government as a poor relation when it comes to funding. They have also campaigned for a senior minister of tourism, such as most other countries have already, with real power to promote and develop the industry. Hope remains that the important role of tourism in Britain will yet be recognised: Robert Key, MP, under-secretary of state at the Department of National Heritage, gave a hint that this new ministry was considering positive action. Speaking at the Tourism Society Annual Dinner, 1992, he said:

> People come to the UK for all the things which we [i.e. the Department of National Heritage] are now responsible for under one roof. This common thread of tourism running through everything is critically important. We are reviewing it. We are trying to see whether there are new ways in which we can make tourism interact with all the other policy areas.

The main objective of the ETB was originally to encourage British people to take holidays in England. Since 1991, however, the ETB and BTA have worked more closely together, as the BTA is scaling down its British operations in order to expand its overseas promotions and reduce costs at the London base. The agencies are now usually referred to jointly as BTA/ETB and they have the same chairman. Because of the growing importance of the industry and the country's entry into the European Single Market in 1993 there is now an even better case for an improved government strategy towards British tourism.

Other tourism-related bodies

Apart from the tourist boards, there are other national bodies that rely on government money to continue their work. The Arts Council, the Sports Council, the Countryside Commission, the British Waterways Board, the Forestry Commission and the National Parks Commission are all examples of organisations whose work involves both professionals and volunteers. The efforts of such bodies are closely related to the success of tourism.

English Heritage (EH) is a good example of the working of a government agency and its dependency on the state of the national economy. When the Department of National Heritage was set up in

1992, it looked at English Heritage (established 1984) and decided that on its budget of £102 million it was noticeably overmanned, overpaid, inefficient and not responsive enough to the demands made on it by the general public. Jocelyn Stevens became the new chairman of EH in 1992, and was given the task of reducing costs and improving services. In an interview with the *Mail on Sunday* (1993) he gave a useful summing-up of the role of EH:

> We protect the fabric of the nation. We are talking about the value of history in the public psyche and also heritage as the prime reason why tourists come here. It means the man-built landscape, industrial buildings, battlefields, ships and docks, barracks, historic gardens, post-war buildings, schools ... there is no end to it.
>
> Take the archaeological task of looking after monuments. There may be some 600,000 archaeological sites in England ... the cathedrals, 62 of them ... consider the 33,735 ecclesiastical buildings ... and then the historic houses – there are altogether 500,000 listed buildings in England. A billion pounds would not be enough.

Such considerations meant that priorities had to be redefined and narrowed down. Resources will now probably be concentrated mainly on major responsibilities (such as Stonehenge and Kenwood House). Less money will be spent on sites which are considered to be of only local importance, and these may be unloaded on to local authorities or voluntary organisations. History was made on 15 June 1993 when the Dartmoor Monuments were the first historic sites to be transferred from the care of English Heritage: a Bronze Age settlement at Grimpspound, a deserted medieval village at Hound Tor, and an ancient stone circle near Merrivale were handed over to local management. All of this goes to show the influence that public audit committees can have on the future of national heritage – and on tourism itself.

Scotland has its equivalent of English Heritage in the Historic Buildings and Monuments Council based in Edinburgh. The council is responsible for the preservation, care and marketing of some 300 historic sites throughout Scotland, including Edinburgh and Stirling castles, the Border abbeys, and the Viking settlements of Skara Brae, Orkney and Jarlshof, Shetland.

Wales is served by Cadw: Welsh Historic Monuments, which has its headquarters in Cardiff. There are 125 sites in the care of the secretary of state for Wales, and Cadw looks after the marketing of historic properties. In addition it has 30 shops for retail sales and trading, as well as dealing with membership marketing (i.e. persuading visitors to subscribe to conservation-related bodies such as the National Trust and the Council for the Preservation of Rural England) and management, market research, sponsorship and fundraising.

Regional and local level

The national boards (ETB, STB, WTB) within the UK system are themselves divided into regions, with regional boards (RTBs) which tend to be orientated towards the commercial and private sector.

Scotland has 32 area boards, including the Highlands and Islands Enterprise, created in 1991 to replace the Highlands and Islands Development Board.

Wales has three regional boards: North Wales, Mid-Wales and South Wales. This reflects the long-held feeling that these areas of the principality each have their own cultural and geographical character; the division is also useful for administrative purposes.

There is a network of 12 regional boards in England. These are non-statutory organisations which have four main sources of income: the ETB, via a grant from the Department of National Heritage; local authority subscriptions; commercial members' sub-scriptions; and sales revenue. Between them the regional boards cover every square inch of the country and look after more than 800 tourist information centres (TICs). The regions are (in alpha-betical order): Cumbria; East Anglia; the East Midlands; the Heart of England; Humberside; London; Northumbria; the North West; South-East England; Southern; Thames and Chilterns; the West Country and Yorkshire. The Channel Islands, the Isle of Man and the Isle of Wight each have their own tourist boards or tourist offices.

The main responsibilities of the regional tourist boards are to:

- have a thorough knowledge of tourism within the region, and the facilities and organisations involved in the tourist industry
- advise the national board on the regional aspects of major policy issues and supply management information
- service enquiries attributable to nationally developed promotions and to provide literature
- coordinate regional tourist information services as part of the national network
- maintain close liaison with planning authorities on policies affecting tourism
- carry out a continuing domestic public-relations campaign with the local authorities, the travel trade and the public

within the region with a view to ensuring that issues are understood and the regional and national objectives known, and to create awareness of the need for tourism to be managed for the benefit of residents as well as tourists
- promote tourism to the region both from other parts of the country and from overseas.

(Source: *ETB Policy Statement*, 1993.)

A glance at the names of the ETB regional boards will show us that in most cases their areas cross the borders of the old-established counties, which are the traditional units of devolved administration in the British Isles. Regions project stronger images than counties as well as being able to give greater technical and financial encouragement. The only exception to this is Cumbria, which covers just the county of Cumbria – though that itself is made up of the two former counties, Cumberland and Westmorland.

In order to grasp how a region is organised to cope with and provide for great influxes of visitors and fulfil the responsibilities set out above, let us take the West Country Regional Tourist Board as a typical example. The region includes the counties of Avon, Cornwall and the Isles of Scilly, Devon, Somerset, Western Dorset and Wiltshire.

How local authorities help

Large, old-established cities like Bristol and Salisbury, which lie inside the West Country region, have established their own tourism boards with full-time tourism officers. In cases like this, and in other large towns, such boards are all the more necessary because of the wealth of heritage involved and the need to reconcile the rival claims of historic areas with the demands of modern developments and transport systems.

Within the region each county, such as Cornwall, also has its own tourist board and its own tourism officer, supported and funded by the local authority. Titles of county and district local government officers vary, but typical job descriptions are: director of tourism for the ... Tourist Board; chief executive of the development board for ...; manager of the ... Tourist Board; tourism and marketing officer for ... County Council; development services manager for the ... Tourist Board; head of marketing for ... District Council; head of tourism and marketing for ... City Council; head of the tourism group, Environment Department ... County Council; head of the Department of Health, Tourism and Leisure ... Borough Council.

Whatever name is given to the post, the responsibilities are for transport and tourism, rural development and/or urban regeneration, planning and research. Local authorities also help by contributing to the finances of the regional boards, and by the creation of attractions, the provision of infrastructure, and environmental improvements. In addition, South East Cornwall has its own *area* tourism office which is responsible for and promotes a number of towns and villages within its special district, for example Looe, Polperro and Liskeard. Further south in the same county, Newquay, Mevagissey, Fowey and St Austell Bay have their own area director of tourism based in Newquay, whilst St Ives and Penzance come under West Cornwall with a tourism office based in Penzance.

Each local area has within it hundreds of hotels, guest-houses, holiday cottages, caravan and camping parks, holiday villages, restaurants, attractions and so on, which pay subscriptions for belonging to the local and regional tourist boards. In return these businesses expect their area to be promoted by and benefit from the advertising campaigns of national, regional and local boards. Some of them will also hope to qualify for an ETB classification as outlined below.

The ETB inspection schemes

The regional tourist boards now inspect over 17,000 hotels, guest-houses, inns, Bed and Breakfast establishments (B&Bs) and farmhouses every year in order to standardise quality of tourism provision. The classifications are: *listed*, and then one to five *crown*, and they describe the range of facilities and services which the client may expect: the more crowns, the wider the range. The grades – *approved*, *commended*, *highly commended* and *deluxe* – where they appear alongside the classification describe the quality standard which the client may expect. Comparable schemes apply to self-catering holiday homes (the one to five keys) and to holiday caravan, chalet and camping parks (the Q symbol with one to five ticks).

Tourist Information Centres (TICs)

The businesses contributing to the regional and local tourist boards will also expect their promotional literature and advertising material to be available at all the TICs near them. When arriving in a holiday area many tourists make the TIC their first stop, looking for information on accommodation (and sometimes facilities for booking), entertainment, attractions and places to visit. Examples of this type of visitor-servicing and marketing structure, which covers an area in great detail, may be found in every part of Britain.

SURE SIGNS

OF WHERE TO STAY

Throughout Britain, the tourist boards now inspect over 30,000 places to stay, every year, to help you find the ones that suit you best.

Looking for somewhere convenient to stop overnight on a motorway or major road route? Look for the 'Lodge' **MOON.** The classifications: **ONE to THREE MOON** tell you the range of facilities you can expect. The more Moons, the wider the range.

Looking for a self-catering holiday home? Look for the **KEY.** The classifications: **ONE to FIVE KEY,** tell you the range of facilities and equipment you can expect. The more Keys, the wider the range.
THE GRADES: **APPROVED, COMMENDED, HIGHLY COMMENDED and DE LUXE,** whether alongside the **CROWNS, KEYS** or **MOONS** show the quality standard of what is provided. If no grade is shown, you can still expect a high standard of cleanliness.

Looking for a holiday caravan, chalet or camping park? Look for the **Q** symbol. The more ✓s in the Q (from one to five), the higher the quality standard of what is provided.

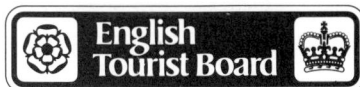

Looking for a hotel, guesthouse, inn, B&B or farmhouse? Look for the **CROWN.** The classifications: 'Listed', and then **ONE to FIVE CROWN,** tell you the range of facilities and services you can expect. The more Crowns, the wider the range.

English Tourist Board

We've checked them out before you check in!

More detailed information on the **CROWNS,** the **KEYS** and the **Q** is given in free *SURE SIGN* leaflets, available at any Tourist Information Centre.

The English Tourist Board's sure signs of where to stay

Wholesale and retail travel

If you were to ask the question 'Who makes tourism possible?' in a busy street or supermarket, the majority of people you spoke to would reply 'Travel agents'; one or two might think about it and say 'Tour operators.' This is really a tribute to the marketing skills of tourism suppliers. The top five UK *travel agents* have maintained such a high profile in town high streets and city suburbs, and have advertised so widely in newspapers and on television that we immediately associate holidays and tourism with their names. The five largest (based on number of outlets) in 1992 were: Lunn Poly Ltd; Pickfords Travel; Thomas Cook; A.T. Mays; and Hogg Robinson. *Tour operators* also have a prominent place in the public consciousness, and the top five (based on turnover) in 1992 were all well-known names: Thomson Holidays Ltd; Owners Abroad; Horizon Holidays Ltd; Airtours plc; and Kuoni Travel Ltd.

The risky and volatile nature of big business can be appreciated if we consider that the top ten operators in 1990 would have included International Leisure Group (ILG), which fell victim to the recession in 1991, and Yugotours Ltd, which has been wiped out by the fragmentation of the former Yugoslavia and subsequent civil war. The average customer of the large, mass-market travel firm does not realise how small profit margins are and how fierce competition now is. Unforseen circumstances like war or the sudden failure of overseas companies can hit tour operators suddenly, and empty seats on aircraft, like empty hotel rooms, are instant loss makers. The general world business scene is one of fluctuating growth and changing patterns of trade; there are few constants. These and other business issues will be discussed more fully in Chapter 4.

Travel agents

These are the all-purpose retailers of the travel trade. The main agents, like those above, have chains of outlets in as many prime sites as possible. They deal with leisure and business travel both within the UK and overseas. Their staff possess all the necessary travel skills and are familiar with the contents of the brochures displayed around their shop; they understand timetables, know the system of fare-pricing and how to obtain tickets for all forms of transport by air, sea, and surface (road and rail). Good travel agents are able, if required, to put together an itinerary, arrange a round-the-world tour, book transport and accommodation or contact ticket agencies to reserve seats for visits to London theatres. In addition they will have kept up with those developments in telecommunications and computing that make up the information technology (IT) on which the tourist and travel industries throughout the developed world rely so heavily. Because of the speed and power of IT, some agencies have 'one-stop booking', through which individual travellers can instantly book their transport to the airport, their flight, their hotel, car hire, a table at a restaurant (plus arrangements for choice of menu), theatre tickets, a night club reservation, or anything else which the tourist could require.

There are also smaller and more specialised travel agents. Some of these deal exclusively with operators who construct 'niche' packages (e.g. study holidays, natural-world packages, faraway winter stays, religious tours and pilgrimages, etc.). Such agents do not have their own outlets in towns and cities, preferring to advertise in newspapers and magazines to reach their clients. Some put together their own packages for minority groups and are, in effect, tour operators. Niches, by definition, can get smaller and smaller, as will be shown in the following chapter.

Other agencies, which concentrate solely on business travel, are sometimes called 'business houses'. Many large commercial organisations are long-standing clients of these specialists and have monthly travel accounts with them. The customers of such agencies are interested in speed and flexibility, and so business houses deal almost exclusively with scheduled flights on major airlines, and usually reserve accommodation owned by the large hotel chains. As noted in Chapter 1, much business travel is concerned with incentive groups or trade missions, trade fairs, exhibitions and conferences. Like the ordinary high-street travel agent, the business house will also put together individual inclusive tours. Tailor-made packages taking in several different destinations are often in demand when trips are made which combine business and pleasure. Specialists apart, though, the *main* business of the retail counter in a travel-agency branch is selling the products of the wholesalers – the tour operators.

Tour operators

Tour operators put together a wholesale package. This means that they must pre-book travel with national and international carriers, charter aircraft, organise transfers from ports/airports, buy space in all types of accommodation, devise a variety of excursions at resorts and provide overseas representation. They then arrange all these elements in various combinations, present them as ready-made holidays in their brochures and offer them to the agents to sell on commission. As in the case of travel agents, tour operators need help from information technology to enable them to negotiate contracts with air, rail and coach companies, and to make reservations for hotels, apartments, and so on. They also need design and marketing skills to put together attractive, informative and truthful brochures. One famous company is so proud of its products that it advertises: 'We don't package holidays. We wrap them up beautifully'.

Many of the big tour operators own or control high-street travel agencies, and also have their own charter airlines. There are currently 650 tour operators in business in the UK alone, so it is not possible to give more than a few examples of the larger ones:

- Thomson owns the travel agency Lunn Poly as well as Britannia Airlines
- the German tour operator LTU bought the travel agency and travel money group Thomas Cook in 1993, and also has a large stake in tour operator Owners Abroad; the combined group own Air 2000, a charter fleet of 48 aircraft which carries 3.3 million holidaymakers annually; it is the first pan-European alliance in the travel industry
- the travel operator Airtours took over Pickford's Travel Agency and the Hogg Robinson travel chain in 1993; in 1994 all the 540 Pickford's and Hogg Robinson travel shops disappeared to become a new travel-agency giant, Going Places, after a multi-million pound re-branding exercise.

The packaged holiday still remains popular, and it should be remembered that not all packages are for the traditional mass market. Holidaymakers have become more discriminating and destinations have changed, as long-haul flights have come down in price. There is a wider choice of group tours for the adventurous traveller than ever before: Latin America, for example, has been opened up in the 1990s as never before to give new experiences for organised travellers. Mexico, Cuba, Peru, Venezuela, Brazil, Argentina, Belize, Panama, Costa Rica, Guatemala, Chile, Bolivia and Ecuador have all now acquired flourishing tourism industries. It is even possible to take an all-inclusive tour to the Panatal region, the remote interior of Brazil, one of the last 'frontiers' to be explored. There is also an 'Amazon Adventure' through the dense jungles of Peru. Formerly, only highly organised and expensive professional expeditions could venture into such difficult terrain, but advances in travel technology and medical science plus newly developed, sophisticated equipment and clothing have opened up such areas to amateur explorers within the last few years.

Tour operators in the UK, North America, France, Germany and Japan provide for a massive sector of the world's leisure travel market, and it is likely that their package products will be in demand for the foreseeable future. This being so, travel agents are also going to remain firmly in the front line of tourism, acting as the interface between the holidaymaker and the industry.

Visitor attractions

The 1980s and the early 1990s were the great boom years for all kinds of historical/heritage venues, entertainment complexes, leisure centres and theme parks. What is more, this period saw an expansion on a world-wide scale.

The 1992 experiment of exporting the successful Disney formula into France is well documented. During its first year of operation 11 million people visited EuroDisney, the new resort at Marne-la-Vallée, 32 km east of Paris, but since then there have been fluctuations in its fortunes. Closer attention will be paid to the problems of EuroDisney during the discussion of marketing in the following chapter.

There is a more unusual theme park that is doing very well in France, though. At Poitiers, just off the Paris–Bordeaux *autoroute*, is what might be regarded as the theme park of the future: called Futuroscope, it is a collection of solid and impressive examples of architecture so modern that they resemble science fiction. Great cubes and crystals the height of a seven-storey building emerge from the ground and house Kinemax, Omnimax and Imax. These are giant auditoriums which use the latest hologram technology and the most advanced stereoscopic projection techniques to produce experiences of virtual reality. There are also exhibition galleries and display halls devoted to the history and science of photography, cinematography and holograms. They are part of a park of the moving image, which includes college and university campuses plus an industrial complex which makes use of the technology on display. Several major French hotel chains have shown their faith in the project by moving to the site, and more than 1,000 rooms are available. Four restaurants of varying levels of expense from self-service to *haute cuisine* are set among lakes. Children have their own amusements, with water scooters, motor boats, an adventure playground and an interactive cinema, where they can join in the plot by pressing buttons beside their seats. Futuroscope opened in 1987 and attracted 255,000 visitors. In 1993 the number had reached almost 2 million. In 1995–96 more than three million customers are expected to turn off the autoroute or make the 90-minute high-speed train journey by the Paris–Poitiers rail link.

Another innovative and up-market venture is the Lost City in South Africa. This theme resort, which opened four months before EuroDisney, is a cross between Kipling's *Jungle Book* and a set from *Indiana Jones and the Temple of Doom*. It was built in the middle of a desert by Sol Kerzner near his other successful resort Sun city, two hours drive from Johannesburg. The Lost City is a high-quality, £150 million project which has covered acres of sand and scrub with exotic buildings, trees and gardens. This remarkable resort hosts the annual Miss World competition, and by attracting the rich and famous it has already become South Africa's major tourist draw.

These are all developments on a massive scale, and great numbers of other themed attractions have been created in countries as far apart as Thailand and Ireland. The following section looks at a few examples of UK attractions, and the number of visitors they have each year.

UK attractions

There were 350 million visitors to attractions in Britain in 1991; 40 per cent of those have been open since 1980, and 60 per cent since 1970. The variety of UK attractions is enormous, for they include all kinds of venues from national institutions to heritage centres and safari parks. Some of these fall into the partially involved sector; some of them make no charge for admission. All are included in the list below because they are so closely integrated into the system of national tourism. The figures shown in brackets represent numbers of visitors in 1991.

- *gardens*   Hampton Court Gardens (1,100,000) Kew Gardens (953,250)
- *historic properties*   Tower of London (2,235,199) St Paul's Cathedral (1,400,000)
- *wildlife attractions*   London Zoo (939,870) Chester Zoo (768,100)
- *country parks*   Strathclyde Country Park (4,220,000) Bradgate Park, Leicestershire, (1,300,000)
- *leisure parks and piers*   Blackpool Pleasure Beach (6,500,000) Palace Pier, Brighton (3,500,000)
- *museums and galleries*   British Museum, London (6,309,349) National Gallery, London (4,313,988)
- *other attractions*   Alton Towers, Staffordshire (2,501,379) Madame Tussaud's, London (2,263,994)

(Source: BTA Public Relations Office, 1993.)

There are in addition many workplace attractions (working environments, industrial theme parks, rural life museums, craft centres, historical and archaic trades, etc.).

The newest and perhaps the most surprising British attraction of recent years was the opening of Buckingham Palace to the public. It seems all set to be one of the great tourist successes of the decade. During the non-stop 56-day opening period in the summer of 1993, over half a million visitors paid £8 per head to see the splendour of the Queen's London home. Comments taken at random from a selection of these first customers were very favourable. On the first day, a queue of about 1,000 people waited for several hours to enter the palace and all agreed it was well worth the wait. The point-of-entry takings were £2.2 million, and the spin-off cash from the sale of souvenirs boosted the total revenue for 1993 to £4.5 million. This sum will be used to renovate fire-damaged Windsor Castle, which is itself a major attraction and was visited by about 2 million people in 1993. In 1994 a new pricing structure was introduced at Windsor, with an overall entry fee of £8 a head. It is, however, the multiplier effect of these prestigious attractions which will benefit Britain as a whole. Trade will be increased for all those who provide transport, accommodation, F & B and other unrelated attractions.

Whether Buckingham Palace belongs to the nation or is privately owned by the Queen is a matter for some debate. However, other venues are easier to classify. Of the current 2,269 attractions in the UK which receive a minimum of 10,000 visits:

- 59 per cent are privately owned
- 29 per cent are owned by local authorities
- 12 per cent are the property of the Government or its agencies
- 59 per cent of attractions charge admission
- 75 per cent of attractions are open for nine months or more.

(Source: BTA/ETB.)

This only touches briefly on a few representative attractions within the British system. The visitors catered for in the UK run into many millions; imagine what numbers would be generated worldwide if the complete statistics for each tourist-receiving country were collated, and you will gain some idea of the importance of attractions to the tourist industry.

Assignment: Investigating a new age of travel

The Channel Tunnel is the most important tourism innovation since the airlines developed cheap jet-travel. In 1994 Britain was connected to the Continent for the first time since the Ice Age. This meant that would-be tourists with fear of flying or the sea – or who just get air or seasick – could now be offered the alternative of going abroad without leaving dry land. The result should be a greatly increased two-way flow of visitors between Britain and the European mainland.

It was estimated that in 1993 18 million people crossed the Channel using air or ferry services. Eurotunnel, the company which operates the car-carrying rail shuttle service, has stated that it is confident of getting 50 per cent of the car market by 1997. The ferry companies have anticipated this great increase of competition, especially since the fares for the Tunnel, ranging from £220–310, are much the same as their own. The ferries have risen to the challenge by offering improved facilities, higher standards of comfort, greater choice of routes, more frequent sailings and smoother, safer 'superferries'. They noted with interest the results of a survey (December 1993) conducted by market analysts Mintel into attitudes towards the Channel Tunnel. This poll of 1,000 adults revealed considerable fear of venturing into the Tunnel:

- only 23 per cent of those questioned said that they were very or quite likely to use the service
- half the respondents were worried that the Tunnel would be a target for terrorists
- more than half were worried about rabies and other diseases reaching Britain through the Tunnel
- 46 per cent saw the Tunnel as a valuable link with Europe, but three out of ten regarded it as 'a waste of money'
- 41 per cent said they were not at all likely to use the Channel Tunnel
- the survey suggested that the most likely British users will be businessmen living in London.

Mintel's leisure analyst, Patrizia Neviani-Aston said:

> We think it is mainly a fear of the unknown which puts people off the idea of using the Channel Tunnel. For many people the concept of actually travelling through the Tunnel feels like something which is still years away, due to the various delays and the media coverage of the controversy surrounding its construction.

Your task is to investigate the actual arrangements made for the health, safety and security of passengers who use the Tunnel. As well as enquiring into the possibilities of accident, disaster or disease, remember that stress and anxiety are also threats to health. Your first step should be to write to: Le Shuttle Customer Service, PO Box 300, Beech House, Crawley, West Sussex, RH10 2YW; telephone 0345 35 35 35. For information on Eurostar (in 'some useful facts' below) call European Passenger Services on 081 784 1333.

When you have obtained as much information as possible, plan and write an illustrated brochure of about 1,000 words, that you think would reassure the three out of four people who say they are afraid of using the Tunnel and also change the minds of those who doubt the service will suit their needs. If you work in groups, you will be able to explore different problems and then coordinate your work. Prepare a talk based on your research which could be given in school or college to an audience who may have many doubts and questions to ask about the safety and security of crossing the Channel by tunnel.

Some useful facts

1 The Tunnel runs from Cheriton, just outside Folkestone, to Coquelles, on the outskirts of Calais. There are three 31-mile (50-kilometre) tunnels: two for trains (one in each direction) and one in between as a service-tunnel and ventilation shaft. The middle tunnel also provides maintenance access – and the means of escape in case of emergencies.
2 It is not possible to drive through the Tunnel. Motorists drive onto the two-tier train in the same way as they would with Motorail or many Alpine tunnel services.
3 The crossing takes about 35 minutes, which is much quicker than the ferry. Only 20 minutes of the journey are actually spent under the Channel. Loading and unloading at either end takes about 8 minutes.
4 It is not necessary to make a reservation. *Le Shuttle* is like a giant conveyor belt. On arrival you buy a ticket, drive onto the next available train and drive off at the other end.
5 *Le Shuttle* is the name of the train which goes constantly backwards and forwards between the terminals. Each train is half-a-mile (800-metres) long and carries 180 cars on two decks at a speed of up to 80mph. Coaches and high vehicles load onto single carriages. Lorries go through separately.
6 According to demand, services run at up to one every 15 minutes. There will always be at least one every hour, night and day, 365 days a year.
7 Tickets are bought at the tollbooth on arrival, or in advance if so desired.
8 At peak times there may be delays of at least half an hour.
9 Getting the car and family safely onto the train is easy: straight down a ramp, through the wide door of the leading

carriage and along several wagons.

10 It is possible to leave your car during the crossing. There is space around the vehicles to get things from the boot, stretch your legs or visit the toilet (every third carriage). There are no buffet facilities and smoking is not allowed.

11 The carriage feels no more claustrophobic than the cabin of an aircraft. It is air-conditioned, well lit and comparatively spacious. Helpful, bilingual crew are at hand to answer queries, and constantly updated information signs show times of arrival.

12 The 35-minute journey is easier and much less stressful than a rush-hour commuter trip on the London Underground. Specially trained guards are on board to deal with any cases of tunnel phobia which may arise. There may be some passengers who develop claustrophobia, fears of a breakdown or of a breach in the tunnel wall. The company insists that such fears are totally groundless and that safety levels will be the most sophisticated on any rail system.

13 Passenger trains will come in with phase 2 of Eurotunnel. The high-speed Eurostar trains will operate a passenger link between London, Paris and Brussels. European Passenger Services will be jointly run by the British, French and Belgian national railways, and the service will eventually slot together in sequence with the shuttle. It will be in competition with short-haul airline services rather than the ferries (see Chapter 5 for more information).

14 There are no plans for these high-speed, city-to-city rail links to carry passenger vehicles, but there will be a freight service between UK and mainland European destinations.

15 Cyclists and motorcyclists have their own areas and special racks allocated to them.

16 Caravans are carried along with cars (there are likely to be strict regulations about the transportation of LPG, Calor Gas, propane, butane, etc., through the Tunnel).

17 Animals are not allowed to travel on the trains unless they go through the proper quarantine procedures.

18 Unlike the ferries, prices are calculated per vehicle, not on the number of passengers in the cars. In addition, the same fare is paid regardless of the length of your vehicle. Minis and Cadillacs pay the same.

19 If the train should break down in the middle of the crossing, at least it will not drift or sink like a ferry, or crash to earth like a plane. Each shuttle has a pair of engines, able to push or pull the train; if they fail there are back-up engines on standby.

20 The shuttle can operate under the most extreme weather conditions. Unlike ferries and airlines, fog, gales, storms and snowfalls will not affect the crossing.

The Channel Tunnel and Le Shuttle train

4   How is tourism marketed?

The marketing of tourism, travel and hospitality, which are both industries and services at the same time, poses more problems than, say, the marketing of refrigerators or audio equipment. Introducing and selling a new brand of breakfast food or soap powder is straightforward compared to the difficult task which faces those responsible for marketing the multiple combinations of accommodation, food and drink, leisure facilities and travel arrangements. These are the raw materials which constitute the finished tourism product. Hundreds of thousands of beds in hotels, aparthôtels (*see* Case Study 2 on Biarritz), inns, guest-houses and self-catering accommodation (villas, apartments, chalets, etc.) are 'bought' in bulk by the tour-operator wholesaler. Millions of airline seats, ships' berths, rail and coach seats are reserved to be sold on eventually by the travel-agent retailer.

The difficulties of forward planning

What makes the situation so difficult for tour operators is the fact that their world-wide planning, negotiating, bargaining and buying-in has to begin so far in advance of the sale of the product. Planning for summer 1995, for instance, began in October 1993. Within a two-year time lag many factors can arise which might ruin the operators' plans: currencies, international interest rates and fuel costs constantly rise and fall; in industrialised countries recessions come and go, bringing about variations in consumer spending-power; wars, terrorist activity, natural disasters and health scares make certain destinations no-go areas. There are many other negative factors which can affect the efforts of tourism suppliers, and the world's press is never slow to exploit a 'Holiday Horror' story. In the same way, television cameras appear from nowhere in response to reports of aircraft crashes, coaches plunging down mountains, *Autobahn* accidents, rail collisions or exploding gas tankers. High-profile reports of such events give a long-lasting damaging image to the whole industry. Just a few examples taken from the many unpleasant happenings of 1993 will help to make this point.

A troubled year: 1993

Tourists are easily scared away even from well-established destinations, and some extremist national groups deliberately exploit this fear by targeting foreigners in campaigns of violence. This was seen in 1993 when the whole tourist industry of Egypt was temporarily wiped out by the attacks of Islamic militants on tourists in buses and ships, city streets and hotels.

In the same year, the Kurdish rebels in Turkey did tremendous damage to that country's developing holiday industry by kidnapping and harassing tourists in the eastern region. Within weeks 50 per cent of the bookings from Germany, Scandinavia and Austria were cancelled.

Even more damaging were reports of disease epidemics. In 1993 Russian television news focused on health problems in the former Soviet Union. Detailed reports appeared in the world's press of 4,000 cases of diphtheria, 60 cases of anthrax poisoning, a resurgence of tuberculosis, outbreaks of cholera and even cases of bubonic plague (the Black Death of the fourteenth century). Thomson, Britain's largest tour operator, suspended trips to Russia for a time, and similar action by other companies followed as a result of customer cancellations. Years of diplomatic effort, beneficial international business negotiations and financial investment were swept away overnight.

The area worst affected by negative publicity in 1993 was the 'sunshine state' of Florida. Ten tourists were killed and dozens of others injured in muggings. Due to detailed newspaper reports, thousands of visitors either cancelled their holidays or switched to other US destinations in California. The Florida Division of Tourism called the situation 'catastrophic'. Officials initiated a massive increase in the number of uniformed officers, removed rental tags from hire cars and issued a security-information pack to visitors. Florida makes $31 billion a year from its tourist industry, and much of this comes from the nine million Britons who travel there each year. 'Incidents like this rip our soul as well as our cheque books,' said state commerce secretary, Greg Farmer, 'But this isn't a marketing problem. This is a crime problem and we need to deal with it.'

The unique nature of the tourist product

It has been said that the whole leisure industry is now totally commercialised and that the selling of holidays must be as ruthless as the selling of anything else. Certainly competition in the industry is as intense as in any other, as may be seen by the feverish price wars and business failures that have become common in the travel trade. The purpose of any business organisation is to make a profit, and making a profit is dependent upon making a sale. Modern retailing methods, along with much journalism and media activity, are geared towards consumerism, and tourism depends upon clever merchandising as much as any other profit-making concern. Only when the product itself is considered do the differences in the tourist industry become apparent.

There are two important questions which must be asked:

1 If we live in a consumer society and tourism is a consumer industry, what exactly is its end product?
2 What precisely is consumed in tourism's production?

These are not easy questions to address. The first one will be answered briefly here, and a fuller answer to the second one given in the following chapter.

It might be said that the product of a holiday should be a dream fulfilled, an ambition realised, a customer satisfied. The same thing could also be said about the purchase of a family car – the cost of which could be about the same as a good-quality family holiday to a long-haul destination. The cost of a 'dream cruise' might well be more. Any kind of holiday, though, is an intangible commodity which, unlike a new car, cannot be examined and tried out before it is bought. Nor can it be used again and again, adjusted or part-exchanged. If anything goes wrong with the tourism product it is much harder to make amends than in other industries.

Negative factors affecting tourism

A two-week holiday which has been anticipated and worked for over 50 weeks of the year cannot be repaired instantly or replaced on the spot like a faulty dishwasher. Disappointed customers will be more bitter than purchasers of other products. Without doubt, they will have lost valuable opportunities, time, leisure, and expectation – and possibly lost face as well. Instead of bringing home a relaxed and fulfilled family with a store of happy memories and a sense of healthy well-being, the dejected victims of a disastrous holiday may be stressed by airport delays, made miserable by sub-standard sleeping arrangements and plumbing, or simply physically upset by unsafe drinking-water, and unfamiliar heat and food. This is the frequent, unfortunate result of selling tourism too energetically and too glibly.

Sometimes the fault lies with the tour company whose brochures do not tell the whole truth about the destinations it is promoting. Too little is included in resort information about how quiet or noisy a place may be; if the area is over-developed; if the infrastructure is sound; if the cost of living is reasonable or not. Optimistic claims are made about distances from beaches and swimming pools that exist only on architects' drawing-boards. Brochures promise flights from regional airports that do not materialise; even the times of departures are sometimes altered without sufficient notice. Last-minute surcharges are made and supplements added without proper explanation.

The EU Package Directive

To be fair to operators it must be said that they are constantly improving the accuracy of their brochures and that abuses of the customers' trust are becoming things of the past. This is largely because of the EU Directive of April 1993 that brochures form part of the contract of sale and must be accurate regarding price, desti-nation, mode of transport, itinerary, meals, passport and visa requirements, deposit required, minimum number of customers required as part of any deal and deadlines for the cancellation of the package. This EU package directive is designed to make the law the same in every member state so that the traveller has the same level of protection no matter where the package is bought. It covers package travel, package holidays and package tours. 'Package' is defined as: 'any combination of not fewer than two of the following: transport, accommodation and other tourist services (e.g. car hire); and that lasts more than 24 hours or includes one night away'.

Any false detail in a brochure and any promise unful-filled by the tour operator will have to be rectified or com-pensation paid. Among other things, the law now requires every operator to protect money taken from its clients. This means that if a company fails, customers who have not yet travelled can get their money back and those that are on holiday at the time do not have to pay any additional costs. Many companies achieve this by being bonded with organisations such as the Association of British Travel Agents (ABTA). A similar guaran-tee is given by the Civil Aviation Authority for operators holding an Air Travel Organiser's Licence (ATOL). Each licence has its own individual number and is an absolute guarantee of full financial cover in case an air-tour operator fails financially. The Association of Independent Tour Operators (AITO) also operates a scheme which ensures that, in the event of a firm collapsing, all its clients will be returned home without cost to themselves.

These safeguards are very reassuring to the client, and should go a long way towards reducing complaints and making the marketing of tourism easier.

Travel delays

There is another consideration which makes travelling abroad one of the most frustrating ordeals that a family can undergo. Sometimes delays and upsets can occur, and holidays can be ruined by factors that are not of the tour operator's making. Sudden strikes by air-traffic controllers or airline cabin staff can ruin a holiday, as can chaos on motorways, freak weather condi-

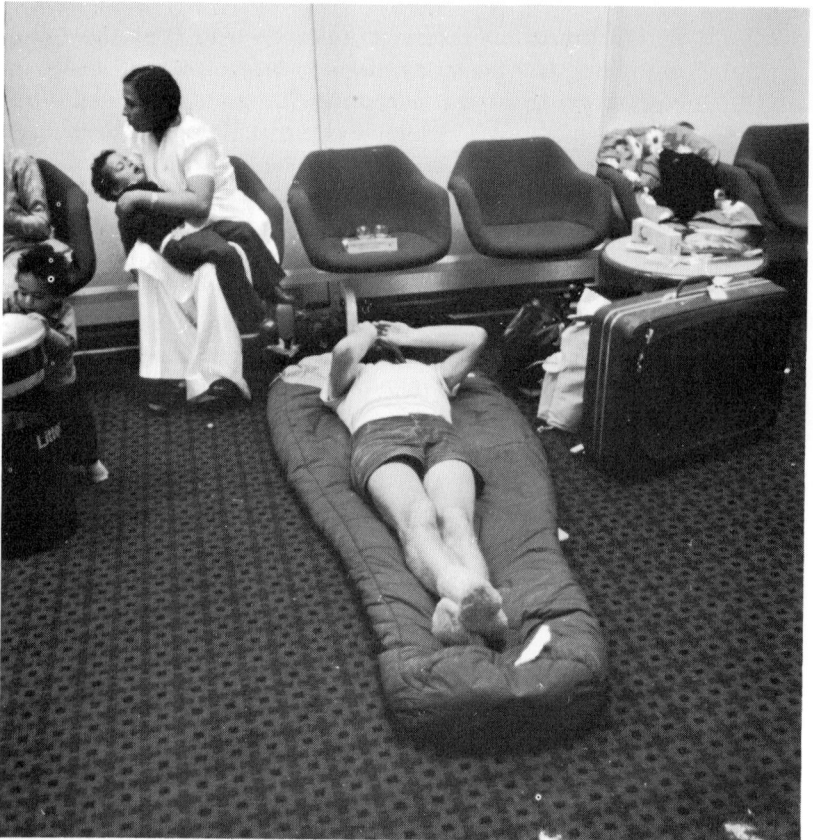

One of the most frustrating ordeals a family can undergo

tions or blockades by pressure groups such as seamen or farmers. These are just a few instances of problems that stick in the public consciousness and hinder the marketing of tourism.

The influence of travel agents

Some causes for complaint could be eliminated with a little more effort from the industry. Eight out of ten foreign holidays are bought from travel agents who, as retailers, receive a commission from the tour operators. Some operators offer higher commissions (12 rather than 10 per cent) to the agents who sell their packages. They also run incentive schemes for those counter clerks or consultants who display their publicity most prominently and sell their product most effectively. The goodies on offer can include travel vouchers, shopping vouchers, generous travel discounts or even free holidays. Travel-agency employees are naturally keen to guide clients toward the products of those firms which offer them the highest rewards. There is nothing legally wrong with this; such inducements to staff are a recognised part of merchandising practice in most industries, and are called a *deal-in*. Sometimes the deal-in is dependent on the agent accepting a minimum number of a certain operator's packages.

The *deal-out*, on the other hand, offers incentives to customers, such as short-term price reductions, low deposits or extra free weeks of holiday. Such promotional offers are tempting to customers who drop into a high-street travel shop, and they are sometimes used to move cheap packages that have not sold well. Manufacturers/wholesalers realise that point-of-sale personal selling is a very potent way of marketing their product and encourage counter staff to push their own brands. Unfortunately, the result of this policy is that many customers are persuaded to buy holidays which do not suit their requirements. After all, an extra week of holiday in a place you hate is not much of a bargain! Every year the complaints department of ABTA has piles of letters expressing dissatisfaction and disappointment. Often this is the result of clients having been sold holidays which are simply not suited to their particular needs, dealing the reputation of tourism another blow.

Irresponsible customers

On the other hand, the dreams and demands of clients are not always realisable or reasonable. At the ABTA's convention in Majorca in May 1993 British tourists were described as the biggest 'moaners abroad'; some holidaymakers were even accused of 'trying

it on'. Examples were cited of groups who benefited from a fortnight in the sun and then put in a false claim for compensation.
Another family booked a trip to an aqua park and then complained
that they had not been told to take swimming gear! The directors
of several travel companies said that they were determined to operate a 'firm but fair policy designed to weed out the whingers and
the simply dishonest.'

The creation of a good image

One way of marketing tourism is to formulate a company policy
which relies on good image creation through consistently providing
quality and value for money. Staff must be educated so that they
are able to advise with confidence and sincerity; ways of organising
and discussing tourism must be carefully considered. The media
constantly respond negatively to the very word 'tourist'. They erro-
neously assume that tourism, mass tourism, holiday tourism and
package tourism are all the same thing; the fast-growing market in
flight-only and independent travel is hardly mentioned. In the face
of this constant misrepresentation, it is little wonder that the
industry sometimes feels unloved. Members of the public and
politicians all over the world eventually come to believe what they
read in the newspapers, which undermines the credibility and
respectability of the whole trade.

Loosening the wrapping

Holidaymakers, as well as business travellers, wish to be treated
as individuals, but they seldom are. Greater flexibility is needed in
the packages offered by tour organisers. In the boom of the 1960s
and '70s, when the novelty of cheap foreign holidays together with
improved travel technology and rising standards of living ensured
that there was a seller's market, tourism tended to be *producer
dominated* or *producer led*. That is to say the package was tightly
wrapped and offered to the client on a take-it-or-leave-it basis.
Some organisations have now taken notice of what their customers
want and try to offer services which meet their demands: this is
what is meant when a product is referred to as being *consumer led*.

British Airways

British Airways is striving to hold a premier position in the
transatlantic flight and holiday business in the face of fierce competition from several tour operators and other airlines such as

Virgin. In addition to being simply carriers, BA is now a tour operator in its own right. It is trying to attract the upper end of the travel market, by offering the greatest possible balance between independence and the provision of all that is necessary to ensure a trouble-free holiday. To supplement its Independent Fly Drive, Fly Cruise, Pre-Bookable Hotels and Hotel Voucher schemes, British Airways Holidays has now developed Tailor Made Holidays, and says:

> In spite of our efforts to include everything that anybody could possibly require in the way of holidaymaking in the USA, we at British Airways Holidays realise that it is impossible, even for us, to feature holidays in our brochure to suit every taste.
>
> **Freedom and flexibility**
> We appreciate that some people demand that extra freedom and independence ... you might want to travel on a different day, or combine different elements of our brochured holidays, for example add a stay in New York or perhaps a four-night cruise to Mexico ... the possibilities are endless! Whatever your needs – we will try to satisfy them.
>
> **Personalised service**
> Our specialist team in Tailor Made Holidays offer a personalised service second to none! With a wealth of knowledge and experience, they'll be happy to make suggestions or recommendations on your chosen holiday, and will provide price quotations as quickly as possible.

This is good marketing, because BA Holidays' planners have put themselves in the position of the customer and tried to see their own product through the eyes of potential buyers. The customer will make a purchase more readily if he or she is treated as an individual, and in order to please individuals BA Holidays has had to research and thoroughly analyse the motivation of tourists and their decision-making processes. In no other industry is a customer-based approach more essential. The quality of service and the quality of management are crucial, and BA Holidays has made considerable steps in the right direction by personalising what is, after all, a package holiday.

Kuoni

The marketing of world-wide long-haul holidays to exotic destinations presents even more pitfalls. In the first place the product costs more; in the second the bewildering variety of countries scattered all over the globe poses the difficult problem of how to provide tailor-made holidays at package-tour prices. For 25 years

Kuoni (founded in Switzerland in 1906 by Alfred Kuoni) has been the market leader in this sector, offering quality and personal attention at competitive prices. Kuoni's answer has been to harness the power of information technology to give an almost unbelievable choice of destination, price level, type of holiday, and air-, rail or shipping line. Their brochure reads as follows:

Flexibility

When you're choosing your faraway holiday it's frustrating if you can't find the one that's just right for *you*.

With Kuoni's revolutionary approach to flexibility, that won't ever be a problem as our sophisticated computer system (which is nicknamed Kudos) allows you to create a unique 'custom made' holiday tailored specifically to your requirements.

It has instant access to literally thousands of airline seats, tours and hotel beds which gives us the flexibility to amend most published holidays in seconds. Add to that our dedicated team of specialists who know every destination inside out, and who provide good old-fashioned experience and advice and you have an unbeatable combination. No other tour operator can offer you such flexibility and choice.

Marketing and information technology (IT)

Developments in telecommunications and computing have created IT, and improvements to the power and range of the systems used are made almost daily. A good computer system can hold vast quantities of data – 50 to 100 million fares for example – and can handle over 2,000 transactions a second. Travel agencies have access to the Central Reservation Service (CRS) and its database. Indeed, in international tourism there are increasingly massive central databases linked by way of advanced communications to hundreds of thousands of suppliers and selling agents all over the world. These international CRS systems are designed to provide world-wide accessibility to the whole tourist industry, making the possibilities for extending and speeding up the process of marketing endless. It must also be admitted that these systems, which display availability instantly and can make on-the-spot reservations complete with a ready-to-sign print-out, give the customers less time to change their minds before committing themselves to expensive purchases.

Most large tour operators and airlines have individual access to computer systems which travel agents can use to check availability, take options and confirm bookings on screen while the customer watches. For instance, British Airways uses PAL Viewdata, Virgin uses Viewdata, Istel 72 and Fastrak VIR while Owners

Abroad uses Istel 41 and Fastrak FAL. Horizon (a part of the Thomson organisation) has TOP, its own computerised reservation system.

Technology of any kind is, however, only a tool – something to make a task easier and quicker to complete. It is the intelligent application and accurate operation of IT which makes it effective. This in turn means that there must always be a supply of well-trained and capable operators to ensure the success of the system. For this reason Kuoni do their utmost to maintain quality control, and promise:

> From the managing director down, everyone at Kuoni is dedicated to constantly monitoring and improving our high standards. Brochure descriptions of hotels and resorts are checked meticulously and 'honest' photographs used to give you the most accurate picture possible of your holiday. We can't stop things changing during the 16 months life of this brochure, but we will endeavour to advise you of any significant changes as soon as we are aware of them.

What is marketing?

The above examples show that some firms have learned from their past mistakes and the mistakes of their competitors to find ways of improving the service offered by the tourism industry, and have contributed much to the improvement of its image. They are managing, in fact, to live up to the old description of marketing as 'the art of making it easy for the customer to say yes'. However, a fuller definition is needed to understand how tourism can continue to be sold successfully, while maintaining the good image that leads to repeat business. The following is quite useful:

> Marketing is getting the right goods (or services) in the right place at the right time and making a profit out of the operation.

Or, more simply:

> Marketing is matching markets and products to the satisfaction of customers and at a profit.

These definitions give us an idea of what marketing is, but they do not tell the whole story. Marketing is all-embracing. It is concerned with every aspect of the product right from the first idea through all the complicated stages of design, market research, pricing, distribution, selling and promotion, until it reaches the consumer. It must also ensure customer satisfaction through after-sales follow-up and enquiries about quality.

Marketing is based on the strategic use of carefully assembled facts. The most important of these facts are the ones about the customers – their likes and dislikes, their attitudes, the changing conditions which affect their choices of product, their spending power, fluctuations in their numbers and so on. All this information can be found in the statistics provided by market research.

Market research

For anyone interested in people, market research is a fascinating study. If history helps us to understand the past, market research helps us to explain present situations and predict future trends. Two main methods are *desk research* and *field research*.

Desk research

Desk research can be done without leaving the office. There are vast amounts of statistics prepared by government departments, trade associations, market-research organisations, trade periodicals, the financial press and consultants. They will either sell information that they have collected independently or undertake to produce individual surveys to the order of specific firms. Some British bodies, like the Joint Industry Committee for Tourism Statistics (JICTOURS), draw their members from the ranks of government departments, tourism suppliers, academic bodies and private consultants. The publications of JICTOURS, which deal with the specification, analysis, interpretation and dissemination of data required for policy formulation, development and marketing purposes, are required reading for anyone involved in tourism. The US Travel Data Center, in America, and the Japanese Overseas Travellers Index in Japan, are designed to monitor travel movements to and from their own countries.

Not all statistical information is collected for business purposes. In 1991, for instance, a new initiative was instigated by the Tourism Society to collect, collate and improve tourism statistics, gathering information from all sectors, including the Government, commercial users in the industry and tourist boards. The Tourism Society is not a commercial body but an independent association which seeks to enhance professionalism in tourism. It is part of the support sector, and its purpose in gathering information is to monitor tourism activity in an unbiased way and obtain a detached overview.

Of all desk research, the most important is a study of the company's own records – customer accounts, turnover figures, sales figures and so on. These will give models of seasonal fluctuations and insights into buying patterns. The second most important form of desk research is to try to study similar figures for the firm's nearest competitors in order to get an idea of what they and their customers are doing. It is impossible to discuss the work of all the bodies, national and international, which collect and process tourism data suitable for desk research. As an example, though, it will be useful to look at some of the information and a few of the services provided by the BTA's international marketing division.

Marketing Britain

The British Tourist Authority has a network of offices and representatives in 27 countries world-wide, servicing 1.6 million enquiries per year about visits to Britain from the public and trade, via the mail, telephone, fax, telex and personal callers. The marketing division collects and publishes statistics annually on incoming traffic from all over the world, along with a brief comment on the nature of the market covered in The British Tourist Authority Marketing Guide. There are seven regions: the Americas and South Africa; Asia and the Pacific; the Nordic region and the Republic of Ireland; Northern Europe; Southern Europe; Eastern Mediterranean, Central and Eastern Europe; and Middle East, Africa and Turkey. A look at the statistics for two of these regions from the 1993–94 edition of the *British Tourist Authority Marketing Guide* will show how valuable the information is.

The Americas and South Africa: 1991 figures				
Country	No. of visits (1,000s)	World total (%)	£ spent (millions)	World total (%)
USA	2,250	13.5	1,275	17.8
Canada	521	3.1	221	3.1
Latin America	197	1.2	137	1.9
South Africa	175	1.1	135	0.4

North America represents 17 per cent of Britain's overseas visitors and 21 per cent of earnings. North America is moving out of recession and the US dollar has strengthened remarkably against the pound, offering great value for money for US visitors to Britain. 1993 looks set to be a good year particularly for value for money products.

Latin America's high spending markets seem set for a resurgence of travel to Europe from which selected British products can benefit.

South Africa presents a resilient market with an excellent regional spread profile and demand for value for money products.

Southern Europe: 1991 figures				
Country	No. of visits (1,000s)	World total (%)	£ spent (millions)	World total (%)
France	2,292	13.8	457	6.4
Italy	714	4.3	383	5.3
Spain	619	3.7	291	4.1
Portugal	100	0.6	53	0.7

Britain's number two market, France, has a wide range of segments interested in Britain ranging from school group travel and language tuition to sophisticated culture, sports enthusiasts and business travel.

Visitors from Spain Italy and Portugal are keen to improve their English, and also relish the appeals of London and the uniquely British lifestyle of the country, especially Scotland.

Field research

Desk research is a valuable preliminary to the formulation of marketing policies. However, in order to keep closely in touch with the thinking of former, current and potential customers field research is essential, and the most important element in consumer sampling is the construction of a good questionnaire.

Questionnaires

In drawing up a questionnaire there are three main considerations.

1 The general subject of the survey. For a tourist survey, the general title might be 'Holidaytaking Habits.'
2 The classification of the respondents. The subdivision and classification of respondents could be:

a) sex? b) age? c) marital status? d) occupations of adults in household? e) house owner or tenant? f) use of car? g) telephone number? h) number of children in family? i) age and sex of children? j) income of household?

Some of these questions are intrusive and personal, and yet the answers to them are extremely useful. There is also the possibility that if direct questions are asked, for instance about age or income, untruthful replies will be given. One way of gaining sensitive information is to provide boxes that can be ticked to give answers within a specific range. For example:

Age: 20–25 ☐; 25–35 ☐; 35–45 ☐; 45–55 ☐; 55–65 ☐; 65+ ☐.
Income: £3,000–5,000 ☐; £5,000–10,000 ☐; £10,000–15,000 ☐; £15,000–20,000 ☐; £20,000+ ☐.

The occupation of the respondent is usually a good guide to spending power, but the questions should be sensitively phrased. Remember also that in any household there may be more than one person who brings in an income. You should therefore either ask 'What is the occupation of the largest income earner in your household?' or 'What earnings group does your total family income fall into?' The following list is often used:

Economic Status
Which of the following best describes your situation?
a) full-time paid work **b)** part-time paid work **c)** full-time home/child care **d)** full-time education **e)** retired **f)** unemployed **g)** other

If the answer to the above question was full- or part-time paid work, which of the following best describes your occupation?
a) professional/senior management **b)** manager in business
c) administrative/clerical **d)** manual **e)** housewife **f)** student
g) retired **h)** other

Type of Household
Please indicate which best describes your household:
a) single parent with one dependent child **b)** single parent with two or more dependent children **c)** couple and one dependent child
d) couple and two or more dependent children **e)** couple, no children **f)** related adults only **g)** unrelated adults only **h)** single
i) other

3 Questions designed to establish precisely the information required. The best questions are those which can be answered by 'yes' or 'no'. Market researchers call these *dichotomous questions*, and they make the work of interviewing much easier as well as simplifying the processing of results.

A useful first question would be: 'Did you go abroad last year?' If the answer is 'Yes', then the interviewer can ask a *multiple-choice question*:

> What was the purpose of your visit?
> **a**) holiday   **b**) business   **c**) visit to friends or relatives   **d**) study
> **e**) other

Whatever the reason given, the interviewer can then proceed to ask:

> When you went abroad last year, did you travel by:
> **a**) charter flight   **b**) scheduled flight   **c**) fly/drive   **d**) boat and coach
> **e**) boat and car   **f**) boat and rail   **g**) hovercraft and car
> **h**) motor-cycle or bicycle   **i**) hitch-hiking   **j**) cruise?

A useful further question is:

> Given the choice, how would you prefer to cross the Channel?
> **a**) Channel Tunnel   **b**) ferry   **c**) hovercraft   **d**) other

This could be followed by a set of further questions about countries/regions visited, type of accommodation, length of stay, cost of the holiday and so on. If the answer to 'Did you go abroad last year?' is 'No', a set of multiple-choice questions can be asked about means of transport, destinations, length of stay and type of accommodation in Britain.

The way in which a holiday was paid for is of great interest to travel agents, tour operators, banks and credit-card companies, and a good survey should ask:

> How did you pay for your last holiday?
> **a**) cash
> **b**) cheque
> **c**) credit card
>
> Which of the following payment methods did you take on your last holiday?
> **a**) travellers' cheques   **b**) sterling   **c**) Eurocheques
> **d**) credit/charge cards   **e**) foreign currency

The most difficult type of question for getting a good result is the *open-ended question*, as it requires more explanation from the interviewee and more time-consuming writing on the part of the interviewer. An example of an open-ended question might be: 'Why did you not take a holiday last year?' One way around this problem is to have a set of alternative statements and a range of boxes that can be ticked off quickly, for example:

> *Statement:* My holiday rarely lives up to my expectations.
> *Alternatives:* **a**) Definitely agree **b**) Tend to agree **c**) Tend to disagree **d**) Neither agree nor disagree **e**) Definitely disagree

Using this system, many statements that would be of use to travel-related suppliers can then be incorporated into the questionnaire, for example:

> I worry about the adverse effects of the sun.
> I would never go on holiday by myself.
> Self-catering holidays are better value.
> I prefer to organise my own holiday arrangements.
> I prefer to book through a travel agent.
> I find advertising useful in helping me to chose a holiday.

Compilers of the questionnaire can devise as many questions of this type as they think are acceptable to the respondent. The answers are easy to give, easy to record and easy to store. Responses to dichotomous and multiple-choice questions are usually recorded on coded forms that can be stored directly in a computer. From these replies statistical figures can then be prepared to provide a wealth of data and information to suit the needs of both large and small operators.

It is also very useful to know which region of the UK respondents are from. Most professional questionnaires now ask:

> Which is your local ITV station? Tick one of the following boxes:
> Carlton ☐; Meridian ☐; Westcountry ☐; HTV ☐; Anglia ☐; Central ☐; Granada ☐; Yorkshire ☐; Tyne Tees ☐; Scotish/Border/Grampian ☐; Ulster ☐; other ☐

Surveys

As well as questionnaires which establish habits, patterns of intention and motivation, there are surveys which measure the level of customer satisfaction. Such surveys are used by tour operators, carriers, hotels and travel agents as a way of monitoring their level of service as perceived by the consumer. Sometimes surveys are conducted by post or by telephone, but the best method is the face-to-face interview which, although expensive, gets the highest rate of response and provides the most accurate figures. To see how this opinion sampling and information processing works in practice, it will be useful to look at some examples of regular surveys and research publications by the BTA:

British National Travel Survey For many years the BTA has commissioned this annual major holiday-industry survey. It provides information on the level of long holidaytaking among the British population, on the number and types of holidays taken, and details of booking, transport, accommodation, destination and spending on holidays both abroad and in Britain.

Overseas Visitor Survey This wide-ranging BTA survey collects information on overseas visitors' behaviour and attitudes by interviewing tourists in all parts of Britain throughout the year. It covers subjects which are beyond the scope of, or not currently available from, the Government's *International Passenger Survey*.

Survey among Overseas Visitors to London This annual survey provides a detailed picture of the behaviour of overseas visitors to London during the summer, their activities and their reactions to the city. The BTA co-sponsors the survey with the London Tourist Board (which publishes the findings) and other organisations.

Tourism Intelligence Quarterly A 65-page quarterly publication which summarises and interprets up-to-date trends in tourism. It includes sections on the state of international tourism, factors affecting the flow of tourism, tourism's contribution to the British economy, tourist arrival and departure statistics, domestic tourism and short- and medium-term forecasts.

Digest of Tourist Statistics A major compendium of facts and figures, including long-term trends, drawn from a wide variety of sources. It includes detailed statistics on overseas tourism to Britain as well as data on British tourism within Britain and abroad.

International Passenger Survey This publication from the Department of National Heritage provides the data from which the BTA produces reports on particular aspects or segments of overseas visitor traffic to the UK. These include: *Overseas Trade Fair/Exhibition Visitors to the UK*; *English Language Course Visitors to the UK*; *Overseas Conference Visitors to the UK*.

Horwath – ETB English Hotel Occupancy Survey These Survey reports, published each month, include measurements of occupancy by domestic visitors and, separately, by foreign visitors at hotels in England.

Advertising

Advertising is only part of a coordinated marketing strategy; it does not sell goods or services on its own. At best it can only stimulate interest, which will have to be turned into positive sales by good personnel, distribution and presentation.

Nevertheless, advertising is powerful and all-pervading, sometimes to the point of being intrusive. Advertising repeats sales information again and again, and it follows the consumer everywhere. The advertising of tourism (among countless other products) is seen on television at home, in pubs, or even in holiday accommodation, where most proprietors now promise 'Colour TV in every room'. Millions of travellers on aircraft, ships and coaches form a vast captive audience that watches films and video programmes broadcasting the hard-sell tourism message in commercial breaks. Commercial radio is punctuated by advertising and travels everywhere with us thanks to in-car entertainment systems. Personal stereos enable product advertising to pursue us into parks and onto beaches. Newspapers and magazines are subsidised by advertisers who pay to have messages about their products displayed on news-stands and pushed through letterboxes throughout the developed world. We see giant consumer images on hoardings in the streets of cities and towns; buses are covered with advertising inside and out; underground railway stations are awash with posters, and the insides of the trains are packed with persuasive pictures and reading matter. When we go to sports grounds, banners catch our eye across track, pitch or stadium and when the participants appear, whether they are on foot, on bicycles or in racing cars, they are decorated with logos and brand names.

High-profile advertising has become a fact of life, and the tourism and leisure industries rely more heavily on its power than producers of many other consumer goods, who sometimes regard tourism as frivolous and lightweight. This is because the ephemeral nature of the tourism product means it has to sell promises rather than objects: it can only deal in offers of fun, freedom or relaxation, natural beauty and man-made wonders, adventure and excitement, luxury and sophistication and, perhaps above all, fine weather. Tourism is usually sold through advertising that puts a gloss and a glow on and around its product. Images from the sunbelt countries can have a very persuasive effect in the chilly cities of umbrellas and overcoats. The optimistic, 'get away from it all', 'fun and sun' advertising that is characteristic of the tourist industry is perfectly acceptable, as long as it is truthful, pleasant to look at and responsible.

In recent years the advertising of tourism *has* become more responsible and informative. As consumers have become more sophisticated they have tended to be less impressed by pictures of busty blondes on beaches. Some have argued that the images of women used in such advertising are simply exploiting female sexuality; in any event, a picture of a pretty woman on a strip of beach, beside a strip of sea, under a strip of sky does not tell anyone very much about the destination being promoted. In the same way, images of picturesque 'natives' in traditional costumes must be used sensitively and sparingly to advertise exotic resorts. Inhabitants of emerging countries do not always appreciate being shown as exhibits in a sort of tourist theme park.

Many operators in the tourism and leisure industries have hit upon a worthwhile idea by becoming major sponsors of sports events, travel scholarships and ecological projects. These give pleasure, opportunity and help to thousands of individuals, and are remembered long after stereotyped images have been forgotten.

Merchandising

Merchandising means all sales promotion activities which aim to generate consumer interest in the product. It goes further than straightforward television and press advertising, and aims to bring the customer and the product closer together. Television and radio travel programmes like *Wish You Were Here?*, *The Travel Show*, *Travelog*, *Holiday*, *The Rough Guide to the World's Islands*, BBC Radio 4's *Breakaway* and others are not advertisements as such. They do, however, stimulate interest in tourism and disseminate information, as well as giving addresses and telephone numbers from which useful 'fact-files' may be obtained.

Travelling exhibitions and showcases are seen at holiday resorts, county shows, flower shows, horse trials and other summer activities, and are very popular ways of establishing liaisons with existing and potential customers. The BBC, in conjunction with the travel trade, holds Holiday Live (the largest international leisure and travel show for consumers) in the Grand Hall, Olympia, each January. All the major National Tourist Offices are there in force, together with hundreds of commercial operators and representatives from the support sector. There is a cinema that shows films of dozens of different countries and hundreds of destinations, along with accurate displays of local costumes, music and dancing. There are even displays of traditional foods and drinks, so that prospective travellers can experience the sights, sounds and tastes of their holiday. On the commercial level, rather than the leisure level, the British Travel Trade Fair is held at the National Exhibition Centre

(NEC), Birmingham each April. Co-sponsored by the English, Wales and Northern Ireland Tourist Boards, it acts as a market place for British tourism and plays host to travel professionals from Britain and many other countries.

The tourism trade makes great use of competitions as a merchandising device. Magazines, newspapers and TV programmes all have their own contests, usually requiring simple answers to win a luxury holiday or other prizes. The successful competitor is chosen by being drawn at random from thousands of correct entries, but the organisers are the real winners as all the entrants, who send in their names and addresses with their answers, provide an invaluable database of potential customers.

Also popular is a system of giving vouchers in those magazines which target age and interest groups with time and money to spare. So, holiday and leisure publications, those targeted at the over-50s and other magazines give such items as coupons for money off cross-Channel fares and car-rental rates, complimentary vouchers for a three-day stay in a hotel (if you buy all the meals there), and two-for-the-price-of-one vouchers for entry to attractions and heritage sites. All these are effective methods of getting details of the tourism product directly to the people who are statistically likely to take up promotional offers and become repeat customers.

Niche marketing

Niche marketing is the sharp end of targeted marketing, selecting a particular market and offering a particular product. Its greatest successes come from the good ideas of innovative tourism suppliers, who realise that there are potential customers with a desire to do something special and unusual on holiday that is not catered for by other companies. This type of holiday is similar to the special-interest holidays that were looked at in Chapter 1, but it is usually more specific in its provision. One of the best examples is the growing market in couples wishing to get married in some exotic location abroad as an alternative to their local church, chapel or registry office. Tour operators are arranging weddings on distant shores for those who wish to 'tie the knot in paradise'. Popular destinations are Barbados, Kenya, Thailand, Malaysia, Florida and Bali. Thomson is currently the market leader and it offers 16 locations in the Indian Ocean islands, the Caribbean, the Far East and the coast of Africa. In 1993 the firm arranged more than 2,000 weddings and they have four full-time UK staff plus representatives in the Caribbean to deal with marriages. The tour operator Cosmos also has a share of the wedding holiday market and its

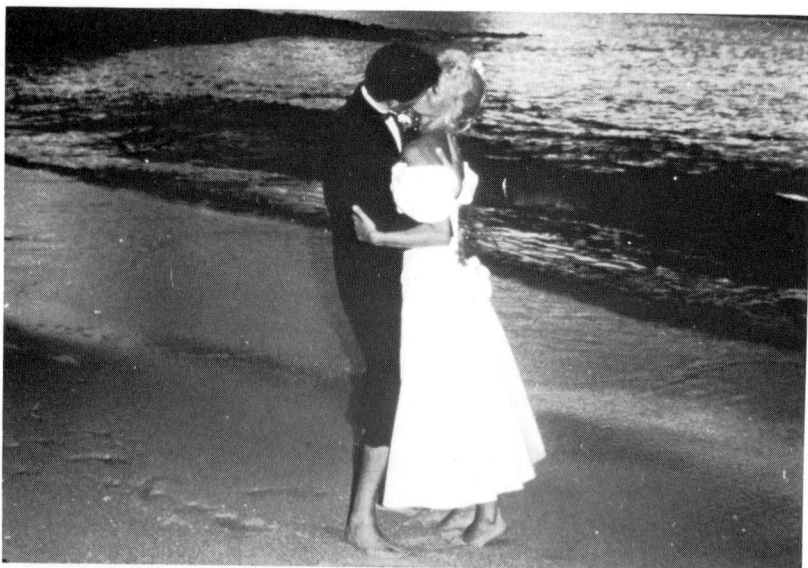

Tying the knot in paradise
(Photograph courtesy of Thomson Tour Operations Ltd)

bookings are doubling yearly at the 10 destinations which they offer. Kuoni too has been quick to make use of its established world-wide operations to fill this profitable niche. It tempts couples to 'Exchange vows on a beautiful tropical island against a backdrop of swaying palms, colourful tropical flowers and a shimmering blue sea.' It is much more romantic to have a ceremony in a beautiful beachside location in the tropics and it also makes good financial sense: the average UK wedding costs about £8,000 but a dream wedding in an exotic location costs well under £2,000 per couple – with the honeymoon included.

On a more homely note, Enterprise Travel caters for the fans of Gracie Fields and George Formby by arranging 'Nostalgic Spring Breaks' in industrial Lancashire. You might think that this location would be difficult to sell, but the organisers realise that it has its niche in history and entertainment, and they urge prospective customers to:

Join us on a weekend of nostalgia. You'll see the landscape depicted in L. S. Lowry's famous paintings ... learn a little of the history of textiles ... soak up the music of George Formby and Gracie Fields! Come with us to Wigan Pier immortalised by George Orwell's book and the music hall jokes of George Formby senior. Explore the 'Way We Were' exhibition, take a ride on the Leeds/Liverpool Canal and see the world's largest working mill steam engine alongside working displays of cotton carding, twisting, drawing and doubling. Come to 'Our Gracie', an exhibition in her home town of Rochdale, and a celebration of this remarkable Lancashire lass.

This is clever marketing, and Enterprise also offers a similar package for Bronte lovers in their North Yorkshire weekend, 'Footsteps of the Brontes'.

Richard Branson, one of the most brilliant innovatory figures of our time in the field of tourism and entertainment, did some market research and discovered that the lure of the Loch Ness Monster nets the Scottish Highlands millions of pounds in tourist revenue from the half a million visitors who flock to the loch every year from all over the world. He also found that Loch Ness is one of the three places that many visitors to the UK, especially Americans, miss because they are difficult to get to (the other two are Stonehenge and the white cliffs of Dover). Branson has already launched Vintage Airways in America, which offers journeys in restored wartime DC-3s and is doing very good business. He now hopes to buy and restore a Sunderland, the classic wartime flying boat, to take tourists on novel excursions to visit and fly over all three out-of-the-way locations, attempting to spot the monster in the course of the trip. Here again is a bright idea which is so unusual it will be sure to find a nostalgia niche in the market.

There are many other examples of good ideas that have been successful – cosy ones like a horse-drawn caravan holiday and upmarket ones like a stay with an aristocratic family in a stately home. Anniversaries of historical events are excellent opportunities for arranging commemorative trips. The Southern Tourist Board ran a campaign to promote the sites of the Second World War Normandy landings which took place in 1944. Southern coordinated a programme of relevant events on the fiftieth anniversary of D-Day after joining forces with the Normandy Tourist Board to work on initiatives to promote the anniversary throughout the UK and the US. One tour operator, Saga Holidays, organised a six-night tour by ferry and coach for veterans of the Normandy Landings and their families. The tour took in sites on the south coast of England and in France, and each veteran received a commemorative certificate as well as a medal from the French government. Saga is now busy promoting 14-night tours of the Vietnam battlefields, which also take in Singapore and Thailand. Not all tour organisers and operators are huge concerns. Some very small family businesses succeed because they offer a chance for the thousands of tourists who want to do something different to fulfil their dream.

Price wars

Even though the tourism product is leisure-centred and pleasure-orientated, the industry itself is fiercely, if not ferociously competitive. If this sounds too dramatic, we have only to look at the price wars of the mid-1990s which followed the recession of the first half of the decade. The big travel companies began cut-throat campaigns offering bargain holidays. One Thomas Cook manager, referring to deep price cuts, said: 'Competition among high-street travel agents will reach fever pitch. Blood will be spilt!' The huge Owners Abroad company pledged: 'We guarantee to match any competitor's prices for the same holiday.' Price cuts of 6 per cent – a total reduction of £60 million – resulted in Thomson selling 250,000 holidays in two days. Their managing director said: 'We haven't merely reduced prices in selected destinations, we've slashed them right across the board. Even in the boom days of the 1980s, we never saw a rush for the sun like this.' By giving away discounts of £3 million, Lunn Poly sold 80,000 holidays in two days with some eager customers queuing for hours outside the company's shops before opening time.

While price wars can be good news for holidaymakers they can give headaches to marketing executives. Price-cutting is one of the most primitive devices in marketing, but it must be precisely calculated. The cost of failure is high: a round of price reductions which are not related to increased sales or decreased costs breaks one of the most basic laws of marketing and will inevitably lead to bankruptcy. As in any other wars, there are always casualties. This applies particularly to the mass package side of the industry which, because it is so capital-intensive, needs high-volume repeat sales to achieve a viable return. Success is dependent on rapid sales growth and the capture of a major share of the market. This is a well-known marketing dilemma when there is excessive, established competition between a large number of companies who in effect are offering the same product.

Brand image

In order to gain and keep a lasting place in the market a good *brand image* is essential, that is the favourable, superimposed 'personality' which is the public's perception of a company. Advertising which successfully presents this image relies on projecting lasting assurances and public evidence of dependablity, quality, efficiency, value for money (the result of correct pricing policy) and friendliness. The brand is usually identified by such elements as an instantly recognisable logo, coordinated graphics, and a bold livery in corporate colours applied to aircraft, offices, uniforms, etc., which must be periodically updated to remain fashionable. The other element is a code of conduct for staff which is developed by staff-training programmes.

To maintain a favourable high-profile presence and retain customer loyalty any business organisation must have good *public relations (PR)*. The purpose of PR is to create a positive impression of a company, ideally one of enterprise, coupled with fair dealing and generosity, leading to success. An organisation must always focus attention on the favourable aspects of its activities.

Negative factors, like those which were considered at the beginning of this chapter, must be dealt with by expert communication. This means that friendly relations have to be kept up with the media, and press conferences organised for the announcement of important company news. PR it has been said, is not about selling; it is about not giving things away! PR executives are keen to see press releases with a positive content calculated to create public goodwill, like those about sponsorship of sport and the arts, contributions to charitable causes, the presentation of achievements and awards, emphasis on child-centred attitudes and support for family values.

EuroDisney

The need for perpetually good PR is highlighted by the troubled financial fortunes of EuroDisney. In 1993 there was speculation in the world's press that the £2.5 billion theme park near Paris might shut its doors over the winter months to stem losses expected to total £210 million during its first year of operation. In the event closure was warded off by substantial price-cutting which drew in a few more visitors. There were also rumours that EuroDisney's proposed new development phase might be abandoned or even that it might close permanently.

Some press reports said that it was high prices and the unreliable weather of northern Europe which had hit trade, causing a consequent drop in food sales and hotel occupany, and leading to a deficit of £4 million a week and a massive fall in the company's shares. A series of press releases attempted to counter any unfavourable impression without actually distorting the truth. In August 1993 Phillippe Bourguignon, the chairman, said:

> As there has been much speculation, the company feels it is important to set out the facts.
>
> There is no question over the long-term future of EuroDisney. The

park is a success, it will remain open for 365 days a year and we are confident that the financial issues will be resolved. EuroDisney is now the most popular tourist destination in Europe. The priority is to ensure that the quality of the product is maintained and the magical experience that has captured the world's imagination since Disneyland [California] first opened its doors in 1955 continues.

He then went on to say that the expansion plans, currently on hold, would get back on track.

Summer hasn't been as good as we thought it would be. Every day we have more than 50,000 people, the hotels are full right now, but July was a bit weak.

Michael Eisner, the chairman of the Walt Disney company, said:

It is monumentally successful with the consumer. We are not the least bit worried.

Later, Bourguignon admitted that EuroDisney was crippled by three problems: a weak property market, excessive debt and slack spending by visitors. He did not deal with the other accusations which have been made. Some observers think, for instance, that Disney, with its child-orientated philosophy and essentially American ethos, cannot succeed in Europe because of inclement weather, bad pricing policies, long queues for rides and opposition from the French, who see the park as culturally alien to their values. Furthermore, in the US Disney has the advantage of experienced English-speaking staff catering for a largely English-speaking clientele.

All of this represents a practical example of the PR rule noted above: 'accentuate the positive and eliminate the negative'.

Awards and seals of approval

These are really an extension of PR work, but they exist within a recognised framework for monitoring claims of quality and value operated by independent bodies. The system of crowns, keys, ticks (for holiday parks) and commendations operated by the ETB, WTB and STB, which help tourists in Britain to find a quality place to stay, has already been looked at in Chapter 3. There are many different sets of symbols used by various organisations to indicate the facilities and standard of cuisine offered by hotels, restaurants and other food and beverage outlets.

Ever since the pioneering days of motoring, the Automobile

Association (AA) and the Royal Automobile Club (RAC) have been using the categories such as 'approved', 'recommended' and 'listed'. They award one to five *black stars* to show intending guests what standards of comfort and service they might be able to expect at hotels and guest-houses which participate in the awards scheme. The AA also gives one to five *red stars* for the very best hotels within any category. Red rosettes (one to five) are awarded to restaurants whose food is of outstanding quality, as well as 'courtesy rosettes' for outstandingly polite service. The RAC uses one to five *red stars* to indicate the facilities, amenities and service offered, and the overall quality of the hotel. Hotels in any category can also be awarded: a white H on a red background for superior hospitality and service; a white C on a red background for extra comfort; and a white R on a red background for a superior restaurant. A 'Blue Ribbon' is awarded to the best hotels in any category. Under the AA and RAC schemes the hotels pay a fee to join plus an annual fee for membership. The various signs and metal plaques are optional but cost extra if used.

Independent guide books rely on personal inspection and/or first-hand reports for their entries. A long-established handbook is the *Michelin Red Hotel and Restaurant Guide*, which lists information on over 4,000 hotels in Britain and others throughout Europe. This guide gives, amongst its gradings, a 'Red M' award to restaurants providing 'less elaborate but carefully prepared meals'. Egon Ronay and Ashley Courtenay have produced highly personal and sometimes rather eccentric good food guides for many years, whilst Johansens has now established itself as a reliable body for monitoring hospitality awards. The Consumers' Association publishes an excellent annual *Hotel Guide To Britain and Western Europe* that gives its most highly recommended hotels the Cesar Award. This prestigious grading is named after the celebrated hotelier Cesar Ritz and represented by a laurel wreath.

The main requirement of any system of classification is that it should be administered by competent organisations and the result of genuine approval, after carefully conducted, regular visits, by undercover inspectors. Awards under those systems which merely rely on an establishment registering itself and paying the required dues are worse than having no gradings at all. The ETB used to be at fault in this respect, but has recently revised its procedures. However, unlike almost every other country in Europe, Britain has no acceptable form of grading and classification which has to be officially recognised by the national tourist office before being displayed in advertising material. Any guide to quality should be easy to understand for visitors from other countries. It should above all be welcoming and user-friendly and state clearly any special requirements (restrictions on dogs, smoking, terms for deposits, etc.) and provisions (such as facilities for disabled guests, vegetarians, etc.).

European standards and schemes

When there are European standards to be observed, systems of awards and gradings are tightened up considerably. The European Blue Flag scheme for safety and cleanliness of beaches was launched in 1987 (the European Year of the Environment). Blue Flags are awarded annually by a European Jury to those beaches and marinas fulfilling 26 criteria, falling into the following categories: water quality, beach quality, and the development of environmental information and education. Winners of Blue Flag awards are highlighted in the brochures of tour operators from all over the world, and there is no doubt that this is one of the best forms of PR, and one that will influence the choice of many families seeking a safe seaside holiday.

The EU issued a Bathing Water Directive in 1992, with the result that Britain will eventually have to improve its standards or be made to answer in the European Court of Justice. The National Rivers Authority (NRA) is committed to improving the quality of bathing water around the coast of England and Wales, but standards still fall below those of the rest of Europe. The Tidy Britain Group presents its own Seaside awards to the authorities in charge of Britain's best-run and cleanest beaches, but it has to be admitted that there is a long way to go before these will equal the Blue Flag standard.

Awards for telling the truth

The Advertising Standards Authority (ASA) says (*Monthly Report,* Jan 1992) that holiday advertising is a regular source of the complaints it receives. The Authority has urged holiday companies to stop giving too sunny a picture of the packages on offer, and says: 'A glance through our reports indicates that there are people in the holiday industry who are ... let us say not as frank as they might be in their advertisements.' Exaggerations and concealment of negative factors can give customers a bad impression, which will mean the end of repeat business not just for the company at fault but for the whole industry. For this reason the ASA wants to ensure that there is no suspicion of dishonesty in brochures that are often the only thing the clients see when making their choice of a holiday. In the previous chapter the powerful new EU package legislation was noted, which must lead to more truthfulness, but the fact remains that not all tourism is concerned with a 'package' as defined in that legislation, and that there really is no substitute for integrity on the part of individual providers. The *Travel Trade Gazette* gives annual awards and trophies for the most accurate travel brochure, for the top hotel group and for other sectors of the industry. This is good PR, especially because the public are reassured when the most eminent tourism trade-journal is seen to be making attempts to keep its own house in order.

Top names in the travel trade also cooperate with the BTA to present the Tourism For Tomorrow awards as part of a scheme to promote more truthfulness about and responsibility towards the effects of tourism on the environment. The attitudes of companies towards conservation are taken into account when presenting many international honours such as the Silver Globe awards for best scheduled airline and best chartered airline.

Customer inducements and innovation

When competition is fierce in a buyer's market, companies must offer something special to potential customers in order to keep their market share. These merchandising incentives can cover a wide range of giveaways, extras and special facilities targeted at specific age groups. It would be impossible to describe in detail all the marketing ideas that travel companies, carriers and agents have devised to attract the customer, and new offers are being made all the time, but here are a few examples of incentive offers taken from the publicity of tourism firms large and small.

Giveaways

Children (2–16 years) go free!
Bottle of sparkling wine and gift for honeymooners and all guests cele-brating birthdays or silver and golden wedding anniversaries.
Free cots.
Free entrance to the casino.
Free golf.
Free tennis court and equipment.
Free traditional Andalusian evening.
Free gym and aerobics.
Free sunbeds, umbrellas and beach towels.
Free entry to our big money prize draw for all who book before May 1st.
Free UK flight connections on selected routes.
All Fly Drive prices include free Collision Damage Waiver worth £100.
Free driving guide and route maps.

Extras

Full Board for all Half Board holidays booked between I and 7 July.
Extra nights – up to a week in some cases.
Low deposit – only £5 per person!
No single supplement.
Extra person offers.
No surcharges guaranteed.
No under-occupation supplement in our apartments.
Bonus excursions inclusive to all who booked last year.
50% discount on car hire.
Fruit, flowers and bottled water provided on arrival.
Big-screen videos in all hotels with regular English films and programmes.
Welcome party and drink; farewell party and drink.
Beginners' Spanish classes.
Christmas and New Year's Eve Gala meals.

Special facilities

Family floor – located on Ist or 2nd floor of hotel. The Kids' Centre for children up to 4 years gives a welcome gift to all babies and offers a variety of children's facilities.
Separate clubs for toddlers and children; children's sections of both pools; playground; playroom; early meals.
Free children's menu for the under elevens.
The Kid's Club means more fun for the kids and more relaxation for mum and dad. We offer to take care of your children with a specially prepared programme of entertainments to allow you the freedom to do a spot of quiet sunbathing on your own, in the knowledge that the children are enjoying themselves in the safe care of our representative.
The Club – the leading specialists for fun-seeking young people. Travel to The Club's action-filled Spanish resorts for sunspots, funspots and nightspots.
Your Leisurely Days Host and Hostess … they're lively and friendly … very experienced … over 55 themselves.
Bingo – Eyes down for a full house! A fun and leisurely way to while away a couple of hours.
Indoor fun – Card and board games, competitions and quizzes, parties, singalongs and much more.
Dancing – Sequence, Old Time, Ballroom and Modern … dance sessions are held at regular intervals throughout your stay.
Singles week – I–8 March.

The providers of tourism go on dreaming up all sorts of ideas and incentives to attract customers, extend their range of travel, lengthen the season and ensure a higher level of service and better value for money. The market is not yet fully developed for, as *Social Trends 1993*, a report published yearly by the Central Statistical Office, notes: 'Four out of ten people still do not take a holiday, a figure that has remained unchanged between the 1970s and 1980s.' Unfortunately marketing people too often devote all their effort and thought to the achievement of short-term aims. This is not always in the best long-term interest and raises issues which will be discussed in the following chapter.

Assignment: Holiday survey

The object of this assignment is to construct a survey which will establish some facts and figures about people's attitudes towards holidays and the way they choose them. Use the notes on questionnaires in Chapter 4 and the list of suggestions below to help you, but add any of your own questions that you think will give an accurate picture of holidaytaking habits. The more completed questionnaires you can collect, and the wider the range of people you interview, the greater will be the value of your findings. You should make it clear at the beginning of your questionnaire that all the information given will remain strictly confidential and only used for the purposes of this assignment.

Some essential questions

1 'How many weeks paid holiday do you receive a year?'
Include tick boxes for the number of weeks ('1', '2', '3', etc.) and a box for 'None'.
2 'Who went with you on your last holiday?'
Include tick boxes for 'partner/spouse', 'children under 15', 'children over 15', 'parent/s', 'grandparent/s', 'other relative/s', 'friend/s' and 'colleague/s'. Make a note of the total number of the party.
3 'How long (in days) was your last holiday:
a) in the UK
b) abroad?'
Set out tick boxes for the number of days ('1–3', '4–7', etc. up to '21+').
4 'In which month did you begin your last holiday?'
List the months with boxes for ticking.
5 'How many short breaks (1–3 nights) did you take last year:
a) in the UK
b) abroad?'

6 'How many longer holidays (4 nights or more) did you take last year:
a) in the UK
b) abroad?'
7 'In deciding your last holiday, who took the responsibility for:
a) getting the brochures
b) deciding where to go
c) booking the holiday
d) paying for the holiday?'
(Set out tick boxes 'self', 'partner' and 'other'.)
8 'Did you have a regular plan of saving to fund the holiday?'
9 'Where did you get your brochures from?'
(Travel agent/tour operator, through BTA/ETB, magazine, newspaper, television, radio, other.)
10 'How far in advance did you book your last holiday?'
(1 year, 9–11 months, 6–8 months, etc.)
11 'What sort of things are important to you when choosing a holiday?'
A typical list might be:
a) weather **b)** beaches **c)** things to do/activities **d)** children's entertainment **e)** adult entertainment **f)** situation of accommodation **g)** scenery/countryside **h)** peace and quiet **i)** art/architecture/culture **j)** heritage/history.
Head your boxes 'very important', 'quite important', 'not very important' and 'not at all important'.
12 'What was the approximate total cost of your last holiday?'
(£3,000+, £2,999–1,999, £1,999–999, £999–500, less than £500.)
13 'Which holiday destinations are you planning to visit in the near future?'
(Africa, Asia, the Caribbean, Europe, the US, regions of the UK.)
14 'What special activity interests do you have?'
(Climbing, cycling, fishing, skiing, water sports, etc.)
15 'What type of accommodation do you prefer?'
(Hotel, guest-house, farm house, villa, apartment, cottage, campsite, caravan, etc.)
16 'What type of location do you prefer?'
(Beach, coastal resort, city, countryside, etc.)
17 'What main method of transport are you likely to use?'
(Charter flight, scheduled flight, coach tour, cruise/liner, motoring, motorcycling, motor/rail, railway, cycle, hitch-hiking.)
18 'How do you prefer to cross the Channel?'

(Flight, Channel Tunnel, ferry, hovercraft, other.)
19 'Do you take any of the following on holiday?'
(Sun preparations, film/photographic equipment, toiletries/cosmetics, books/magazines, maps/guides, beach/swimming clothing and equipment, insect repellent, travel medicines, etc.)

There are many more questions that could be asked about holiday habits and intentions which cannot be covered in a general questionnaire. You could, for instance, try to discover which are the most popular travel agents and tour operators; you could attempt a survey which looked at the provision for people with disabilities and special needs; or you could compile a different type of questionnaire dealing with customer satisfaction about previous holidays.

5 Tourism – a sustainable industry?

Part of the answer to the above question lies in examining more closely what is consumed in the production of tourism. It is easy to make emotional, sweeping statements and say that tourism is a menace, in that it:

- eats up whole landscapes and swallows up cultures
- brings out the worst in human nature, the blatant commercialisation of hospitality making the inhabitants of host areas greedy
- encourages national governments and private developers to become short-sighted and too interested in satisfying their immediate hopes and ambitions
- leads to the pollution of the seas and skies, and the destruction of wildlife in every area that it touches.

There is some truth in all of these assertions, which has led to an anti-tourism lobby that sees the raw materials of tourism as too precious to be gobbled up by the commercial interests of the manufacturers, wholesalers and retailers. Look also, say the protesters, at the consumers. They come in crowds for fixed fortnights and either 'fly and flop', 'cruise and snooze' or 'rush and crush', looking vacantly at things that they do not understand or enjoy. The hosts, say touro-critics, pull down the architecture the visitors come to see and put up blocks of 'battery accommodation' which resemble those that the tourists are running away from. The ordinary inhabitants of tourist traps see their areas overrun and are obliged to live in public for the whole summer. Also, the tourists who pay inflated rates for food and accommodation can have an unbalancing effect on the local economy. The inhabitants come to see tourists not as interesting visitors from another country but as walking wallets to be prised open. The tourists, in turn, despise the inhabitants for being poor, greedy and feckless.

Vague, emotional and irrational attacks on the industry will not solve any problems, nor will they alter the fact that tourism is here to stay and is certain to expand. Chapter 1 highlighted some of the lasting facilities and valuable advantages which the industry brings to all countries – developed or undeveloped – and the way in which it makes substantial financial contributions to a nation's welfare. In this chapter the negative aspects will be examined honestly and realistically. The sensible way to approach the uncontrolled consumerism of tourism is to be alert and plan carefully to avoid overselling and overdevelopment before more damage is done. In other words, it is necessary to anticipate the problems arising from the pressures of contemporary tourism that are so great they can no longer be left to the workings of the market: market forces are wonderful instruments in the short term, but they can create havoc over a longer period. There must be a conscious effort to integrate environmental and commercial objectives, and to consider the size and nature of visitor demand and its impact on destinations. After that, steps must be taken to improve the quality of the tourist experience both physically and intellectually so that hosts and guests develop mutual respect. A high-quality environment is an integral part of the visitor's enjoyment and should be a matter of pride to the host. Attention must also be paid to the safety and welfare of visitors just as a careful host should do.

This is what is meant by responsible tourism which will help to create a sustainable industry that should continue to be welcomed in every country of the world. Similar concepts have been forming in the minds of forward thinkers in all tourism sectors for the past 20 years. As far back as 1987 the World Commission on Environment and Development issued a wise and far-sighted report entitled *Our Common Future*, which defined sustainable development as:

> Development that meets the needs of the present without compromising the ability of future generations to meet their own needs.

In simple terms this means that flexibility and respect for others are needed when initiating profit-making tourism enterprises. It does not mean that the industry's values and attitudes have to stay fixed, while society and technology, continue to change. We are all people in transition. Attitudes do change, and although in most parts of the world tourism ought to adapt to the host environment, other countries should not be discouraged from opting for the changes which tourism will bring in its wake. The industry must work in harmony with resident communities, rather than tell them what they ought to want or try to impose itself upon them.

Environmental problems

The ecological problems raised by tourism development are enormous, but the industry should not be blamed for all the ways in which the balance of nature has been undermined by the actions of our race. The sheer scale of population growth over the last 30 years, due largely to a soaring birthrate and advances in medical science, has led to tremendous pressures on the Earth's resources. The rapidly accelerating pace at which technology has been applied in the home and workplace along with universal demands for a better standard of living have led inevitably to change and development, and the urban environment continues to expand. Consider the following:

- it is estimated that in the year 2000 the world population will be around 6.2–6.3 billion
- the urban proportion of the world's population grew to 43 per cent in 1990 from 37 per cent in 1970; it will reach 47 per cent by the end of the century
- this growth will be concentrated almost exclusively in non-industrialised countries, because approximately 70 per cent of the population of wealthy nations already live in cities; during the next century the population of the poorest capitals will explode
- in the year 2000, 25 cities will have more than nine million inhabitants.

(Source: 'Caring for the Earth', a report prepared for the *United Nations Environmental Programme*, 1990.)

The industry should try to ensure that tourism does not make these and other environmental problems worse. The **areas of concern** are: the impact of tourism on both the natural environment and the built environment, which raises the inter-related issues of erosion, pollution, consumption of resources, wildlife welfare, and respect for heritage; the quality of the tourist experience, which involves fair operation of business principles, opportunities for cultural interchange, arrangements for safety and security, and provision of information and education.

Because these threats to the credibility of tourism have become so closely interlinked, it is difficult to isolate single factors for discussion without referring to others – some of which are not directly caused by tourism. However, the following examples look at some of the more obvious and important issues which are attracting criticism of the industry.

Fragile Earth

Erosion is simply the effect of forces which wear things away. The word is most often applied to the effects of wind, rain, snow, ice and frost upon hills and mountains, as well the action of the sea on coastlines. What is not generally realised is that the feet of climbers, trekkers and walkers can do almost as much damage. A few examples from Great Britain will illustrate this point.

Ben Nevis in Scotland is, at 4,406 feet, Britain's highest mountain. Its peak, however, was 7 inches lower in 1994 than it was in 1984. The tens of thousands of visitors who climb to the summit each year are literally wearing it away. The highest mountain in Wales, Snowdon (3,560 feet), is in an even worse situation. It is being eroded by hordes of day trippers, and these armies of climbers have worn paths into deep grooves. In 1991, a party of Girl Guides walking up the Pyg track from Pen-y Pass were buried when the sides of the path caved in on top of them in a rainstorm. The mountain railway from Llanberis means that more visitors reach the top of Snowdon than on any other peak in Britain. In some places it has been worn away to a depth of 10 feet. This in turn has exposed huge boulders which will eventually roll downhill and do more damage. In holiday times, queues of people form along the narrow crests of Snowdonia, like the Crib Goch, which give spectacular views, and there is a constant stream of large and small stones bombarding the lower slopes.

In the Lake District a strange situation exists whereby paths are being turned into rivers of mud by over-use and are then rebuilt by teams of holidaymaking volunteers. In Great Langdale, Cumbria, it took a task force of National Trust volunteers months to shovel and crowbar the Raven Crag hillside back into place. Staircases have now been built up steep scree, and climbers are routed up a stone-paved path so that the pub and the farm below may be safe from dangerous rock falls. Conservation teams are constantly topping-up the erosion caused by millions of footsteps over an area stretching from Dartmoor in the south to the Highlands in the north. Conservation workers also plant clumps of indigenous trees like holly, oak and rowan in order to bind the slopes together.

On sections of the 250-mile Penine Way, the route is so well trodden that it can be seen for miles. Where it crosses the Peak District hills in Derbyshire, plastic matting has been laid over acres of moorland trampled down into the peat: this is to protect the tender skin of the landscape. Pounded earth becomes as hard and sterile as cement; when heavy rain falls, grooves and streams are cut into the surface, and, because there are no roots to hold it together, it crumbles and is washed away. So much damage is being done to beauty spots in British national parks that a campaign has been launched to urge tourist businesses to help protect the environment and plough back some of the money visitors spend into conservation projects. The 11 national parks in England and Wales now total 103 million 'visitor days' every year and in some months popular areas are in danger of being totally overwhelmed. The Countryside Commission publishes an excellent guide, *Tourism in National Parks*, which urges tourist business operators to aid the local economy of the parks by using local labour and produce to improve information given to visitors and support conservation.

Avalanche of tourism in the Alps

Similar situations exist on what have been called 'the eroding Alps'. The problem in Switzerland is particularly bad:

- 230 tour operators in Britain alone send 750,000 skiers a year to the Swiss Alps
- the popularity of skiing is increasing by about 5 per cent a year
- 41,000 ski lifts capable of transporting 1.5 million people *an hour* criss-cross the slopes
- at least half the trees in Switzerland are dying from pollution by cars or acid rain
- whole forests, which provide protection from avalanches, have been cleared to make way for pistes
- artificial snow from some 5,000 snow cannon are smothering the delicate alpine flowers and grasses.
- 405,000 kms of roads run through the Alps, carrying 20 per cent of all passengers and 15 per cent of goods transported in western Europe
- on the St Gotthard Pass alone, heavy lorries and cars deposit 30 tonnes of nitrogen oxide, 25 tonnes of hydrocarbons and 75 kg of lead into the atmosphere every weekend.

(Source: *The Times*, 23 September 1992.)

The Austrians have similar problems and now actually ration access to certain ski areas at peak periods of the season (Lech and nearby Zurs, around the shoulder of the Valluga from St Anton were the first major regions to do this). They argue that just as a restaurant or a hotel can have no accommodation left, a mountain can also become full. The same thinking may be applied to the camping capacity of beauty spots, and some authorities reason that if the volume of visitors seems a threat to their environment and

The avalanche of tourism

the local population, the answer is to close the valley when its comfortable limits are reached. If this seems a harsh limitation of people's enjoyment, you have only to investigate those situations where tourism is still a mass industry with a develop-and-be-damned attitude. When thoughtlessness is multiplied on a global scale, colossal congestion and consequent damage are caused to landscapes, natural vegetation and animals.

Crumbling coral

Coral reefs are fragile, vulnerable ecosystems which live and grow below sea level. In many tropical areas they have been under sustained attack from development, tourism and natural factors; in some regions (notably the Caribbean) the reefs have been severely reduced or even destroyed by tourism exploitation.

Australia's 2,000-kilometre Great Barrier Reef has been a popular tourist attraction for decades. As well as the damage that is being caused by the crown of thorns starfish eating it away, the coral is also being eroded by human activity: boats bump into it, anchors crash down on it, and thousands of scuba divers and snorkellers break off huge chunks, either as souvenirs or for sale to a flourishing jewellery and tourist industry. When you consider that more than one and a half million people visit the reef every year it becomes clear that they could completely destroy large sections of it unless it was protected. The Australian government, however, has an excellent system of marine parks, which are zoned to prevent over-use and over-development. Some zones of the 350,000-square kilometre Reef Complex allow tourism and fishing, but others are firmly closed to the public in the interests of conservation of the reef.

Australia is now taking conservation very seriously, and on Fraser, its second largest island after Tasmania, a development called the Kingfisher Bay Resort and Village was built in 1993. Though it is a sizeable resort it has been built according to strict guidelines so as to have minimal impact on the island's abundant wildlife. The idyllic surroundings, which include rainforests, freshwater streams, beaches and underwater reefs, are protected by the regulation of tourism activities, and the scheme is intended as a blueprint for responsible tourism in other sensitive environments.

Tainted Earth

Pollution is said to occur when the natural or built environment is made dirty and unsightly, contaminated – even poisoned. Tourism is by no means responsible for all the pollution of land, sea and sky, which today is such a world-wide problem, but it may contribute more than its fair share. As an extreme example of pollution in a remote, inaccessible area, one only has to consider Mount Everest (29,028 feet). After many attempts, this, the world's highest peak, was first conquered in 1953 by a team led by Colonel (later Lord) John Hunt. Since then hundreds of climbers – sometimes as many as 38 in one week – have queued up to reach the top. Behind them have come biologists, naturalists, ornithologists, geologists, sightseers and tourists. What were formerly primitive Nepalese villages have now become lively tourist centres, complete with souvenir shops and bed-and-breakfast establishments, a transformation that has happened over the last 20 years, because of improved transport and access to previously forbidden areas. Tour operators have been quick to capitalise on these developments and the huge numbers of foreigners trekking to Mount Everest, Mount Annapurna, Mount Nanda Devi and Mount Kangchenjunga have caused alarm to locals and governments alike.

In 1986 the Annapurna Conservation Area Project was set up, with the principal aims of sustainability, education and participation by local people. By order of the Nepalese government, every tourist entering the region now pays the equivalent of US$7 as a tax which goes towards community projects and a conservation education programme.

Nanda Devi is in India, 530 km northeast of Delhi. The area around it was made into a national park, and from 1974 tourist traffic was permitted. As a result the land was over-grazed by pack animals used to support expeditions, trees were felled in large numbers to provide fuel, the topsoil was eroded and plant life was disturbed. The region had to be closed in 1983 to allow time for it to recover from the impacts of tourist traffic, and it is not known when it will re-open.

Everest itself has had to take stern measures to deal with the problems of rubbish accumulation and unused mountaineering equipment left behind by expeditions. At 26,000 feet on the South Col Plateau there was a rubbish dump that has been called 'the tip at the top of the world'. Dozens of discarded oxygen bottles and tents, heaps of mountaineering equipment and clothing and even five corpses (all perfectly preserved due to the cold and lack of oxygen) were scattered over a wide area. There was an estimated 10 tons of rubbish. The Tourism Ministry of Nepal fined a British mountaineering team £66,000 in 1993 for sending too many people up Everest. Under new regulations no expedition to the world's highest mountain can have more than seven foreign members, and the 1993 expedition was discovered to have had fourteen. In 1992 a conservation project in Nepal to clean up the Himalayas won the Tourism for Tomorrow trophy awarded by the Tour Operators Study Group, the British Tourist Authority and television's *Wish You Were Here?* programme.

If litter and congestion can be a problem in the Himalayas, what hope is there for more ordinary tourist destinations?

Contaminated waters

The clearing up of litter and rubbish from the surface of the Earth is a simple matter compared to the problem of cleaning polluted water. The last chapter looked briefly at the need for clean beaches to attract tourists to resorts, and mentioned the EU European Blue Flag awards. We need look no further than the seas around Britain to find shocking examples of contaminated waters. In 1993 the *Heinz Good Beach Guide*, produced by the Marine Conservation Society (MCS) quoted some startlingly unpleasant facts:

- Britain pumps 300 million gallons of sewage into the sea *every day*
- much of this is untreated and includes a mixture of domestic waste water, cleaning agents, industrial effluent, storm water and solid litter
- 88 per cent of outfall pipes in Britain still carry raw or 'screened-only' sewage

- 22 per cent do not even have screens to remove solid litter, medical waste and sanitary material
- 74 beaches lost all their recommendations because they did not meet the stringent new guidelines (1992) of the EU Bathing Water Directive.

Untreated or 'raw' sewage contains harmful viruses such as meningitis, salmonella and Hepatitis A which are able to survive in the sea for up to 90 days; medical waste includes soiled dressings, syringes, intravenous drips and blood bags. In 1993 only 19 beaches gained the EU Blue Flag award. To win a flag, a beach must have uncontaminated bathing water; it must also be free of oil pollution, dead animals, litter, industrial waste and decaying seaweed; dogs must be banned in summer; the beach must also have easy access, plus drinking water and toilets within easy reach. To qualify as a Blue Flag resort, shops and certain other seaside facilities also have to be available nearby.

The Tidy Britain Group's own seaside awards (blue and yellow flags) can apply to a newer category of 'rural' beaches which do not have to match the facilities of 'resort' beaches. Unfortunately, the cleanliness of bathing water off such places needs only to conform to the earlier EU Bathing Directive of 1975. Much still remains to be done to remove what has been called 'the tide of filth' from around our coasts.

What is even more appalling is the realisation that Britain is far from being the worst offender in this respect. The Consumers' Association published a report on the world's very worst resorts (*Holiday Which?*, 1992). These were situated in various countries scattered around the world as far apart as Thailand, Tunisia, Malta, Majorca, Greece, Turkey, Portugal, Bulgaria and France. Many of their beaches were described as 'filthy, strewn with litter and bordered by stinking open sewers'.

Many lakes and rivers around the globe are also suffering from serious pollution. They too are turned into streams of poison that threaten inland animal life, plant life and human well-being as they pour down to add to the contamination of the seas.

Unbreatheable air

Air pollution is high on the list of people's complaints about the management of the environment. This may be because the ever-growing volume of road traffic, which is so close to us all, puts petrol and diesel fumes into the air that we can see, smell and taste. Restrictions on the volume and noxious content of vehicle emissions through the introduction of unleaded petrol and the use of catalytic converters have made great improvements to the air quality of American and European urban areas. This benefit is off-set to some extent by the constantly increasing volume of road traffic in developing countries, and it cannot be denied that the tourist industry is responsible to a great extent. Indonesia, for instance, is now the fourth most populous nation in the world, with 184 million citizens, yet it still has to cope with an ever-growing burden of tourist traffic.

All but the most remote regions of the world are now affected by exhaust fumes, and even when using lead-free petrol, poisonous carbon dioxide is produced along with harmful hydrocarbons. Carbon dioxide is an unwanted by-product that has been identified as being partly responsible for global warming, the 'greenhouse effect', which is slowly changing the climate of the Earth.

Acid rain

Pollution in the atmosphere increases the natural acidity of rainfall more than 1,000 times. The burning of coal or oil by industry produces the gases sulphur dioxide and nitrogen oxide; the fumes from motor vehicle exhausts also produce nitrogen oxides as well as the hydrocarbons noted above. The effect of sunlight on this mixture is to create other pollutants such as ozone. Eventually these pollutants react with the sulphur and nitrogen oxides to form sulphuric and nitric acid in the tiny droplets of water that form clouds.

These acids are carried, often for great distances, and fall as acid rain. Over one million square kilometres of European forests have suffered from the effects of acid rain, which is fatal to trees. Wildlife also suffers, because when acid rain pollutes waterways, great numbers of fish and fish-eating birds are inevitably killed. Damage to buildings and monuments is another unwanted effect of this deadly rainfall.

Congestion

Apart from the emissions of dangerous chemicals from the exhausts of cars, lorries and buses, there is the problem of congestion. Picturesque winding country roads, coastal corniches and once-lonely moorlands have all been choked by heavy traffic, which at peak holiday times destroys all the pleasant sense of freedom that personal transport should give. This was formerly a problem exclusive to Europe and the US, but the continuing increase in car production means that very few countries are completely free from the rush and crush of vehicles. Lines of parked cars clutter the streets of villages and seaside towns; famous landmarks and natural wonders can only be viewed through the ranks of parked cars. Because it is a small, densely populated country with a high ratio of car owners, Britain has particular problems in this respect. In recent years the English Lake District and some of the British national parks have had to take measures to restrict access to their areas. Park-and-ride schemes are being tried in areas of outstanding natural beauty to ensure that everyone can enjoy the countryside.

Separating mechanised from muscle Power

The greatest problem is that motor and muscle power do not mix. Cycling, horse-riding and walking cannot be enjoyed where small country lanes have been widened to take double lines of speeding cars. Noise and fumes wipe out the sounds and scents of nature, and there is little time to stand and appreciate the surroundings, where there is a need to concentrate on dodging the wheels of traffic. In recent years specially designed off-road vehicles (some of them hired as part of an organised tourist package) have even invaded bridle paths, tracks and the ancient turf-surfaced green roads once used by drovers. This is a most disturbing development from every point of view.

Center Parcs has proved that, given the choice, people are pleased to leave their cars in the central car park of their holiday villages and transport themselves on foot and by bicycle in an ecologically friendly way. The company secured its reputation in Britain by establishing three villages at Sherwood Forest near Nottingham, Elveden Forest near Cambridge and Longleat in Wiltshire. Their unique blend of country club, health farm, villa holiday and weatherproofed sports and leisure facilities set in hundreds of acres of natural or enhanced wooded landscapes has ensured commercial success and given a clear environmental conscience to both company and customers. The opening (July 1994) of the Longleat village in 400 acres of the Longleat Estate proves that a holiday in relaxing, fume-free, natural surroundings is still highly popular with many families.

Threats to the built environment

The centres of historic cities and towns all over the world are under threat from the cars and coaches of tourists. Bangkok and Budapest are as traffic-jammed as Bath and Barcelona. In fact, the smog, fuel fumes and raucous din of traffic jams have turned these places into smaller versions of Los Angeles: mechanised urban nightmares.

Tourism in Venice

Old cities – the built heritage – are sensitive areas. The same exhaust gases that kill trees also attack old stonework, timbering, ironwork and gilding. Pressure from uncontrolled visitor flow erodes the built environment as well as mountains and moorland, and heritage cities are placed under an intolerable strain by the volume of tourists. Apart from the vibration damage caused by heavy traffic, the footsteps and fingers of countless sightseers make wearing contact with ancient paving and statues, as queues shuffle slowly past works of art in churches, cathedrals, castles, temples, palaces and great houses. Even the accumulation of breath from streams of visitors can pollute the air in museums, galleries and so on, and do irreparable damage to valuable artefacts. The sinking, decaying city of Venice has become so concerned about the threat to the structure of its heritage that on some days, at the height of the tourist season, it declares itself 'full', and closes the city limits.

Controlling the car

Venice might have canals congested with craft and streets packed with people, but unlike most other tourist meccas its central area does not have trouble with cars and buses. Many historic towns have streets and squares which date back to medieval times or even earlier. They were never designed to accommodate mechanised transport and their narrow, twisting thoroughfares cannot be adapted to it without wholesale demolition. Sometimes, by accident or design, cities have been cleared of the legacy of ages past. The disastrous great fire of 1666 wiped out medieval London, whereas the Paris of the Middle Ages was systematically destroyed in the nineteenth century by ambitious architects. Centuries of warfare have reduced others to a fraction of their former glory, but many of the world's great cities and old towns have treasured the heritage of their ancient central areas and have pedestrianised them to exclude the motor car. That solution, though, raises another question. Where do you park all the vehicles that remain when motorists become pedestrians?

Where a total ban on cars has proved impossible various traffic-calming measures have been introduced to slow the flow of vehicles. These range from the chicane – where the pavement curves out to narrow the road; the traffic throttle – where two lanes temporarily merge; the gateway – where traffic has to slow down to pass between pairs of pillars or specially planted trees; small traffic islands; humps of various heights; and rumble strips – lines of granite setts protruding an inch or so above road level. All these artificial 'hazards' help a little: they make life easier for the sightseer and shopper. In addition, traffic which moves slowly does less damage to old structures.

Ever-expanding roads

It must be admitted that wherever tourism has been developed into a mass industry, problems have always followed, and few places are regarded as sacred. Even the British national parks authorities are now planning to initiate tourism projects by establishing craft centres, theme parks, conference centres and other artificial attractions. Roads which give access to beauty spots, historic places and attractions are invariably widened and upgraded, which means that more countryside is covered over by asphalt and polluted by fumes. Worse follows: better roads to any single attraction always result in a flood of fresh planning applications and an eventual increase in tourist-orientated developments such as water worlds, caravan parks, holiday accommodation, golf courses and marinas. This in turn means yet more traffic bringing bigger crowds, more air and water pollution, more erosion, thus causing more problems for the countryside, the architectural heritage, local residents and every individual who wishes to walk, ride or cycle.

The dilemma of the motor car is one of the greatest facing the tourist industry. Tourism is about pleasure and enjoyment, so it makes planners unpopular if they try to curtail the freedom to use personal transport as and when the individual wishes. Restrictions on the use of private cars in Europe and the US would hit commercial interests very hard. Just to take a few examples, what would happen to car-hire businesses, the car ferries, the car-transporting trains of the Channel Tunnel, the booming trade in flydrive holidays and the motor/hotel industries?

Commercial operators are not the custodians of the environment. Remoter British tourist-receiving areas such as the south-west of England and the north of Scotland depend heavily on the private motorist and need wide, fast roads to support their economy. Press advertisements for the Cornwall Tourist Board proclaim:

> ### Now a Short Break in Cornwall is even closer...
>
> ... with the new motorway-style A30 from the M25 to the centre of Cornwall and the Atlantic Highway (A361/A39).

and

> ### Driving to Cornwall? – No problem
>
> ... with the new motorway-style A30 road all the way from the M5 to the centre of Cornwall!

A speedy, easy road beyond the Exeter end of the M5 was clearly much needed for the good of the tourist industry which is vital to the South West. Nevertheless, 'no problem' for some means an environmental headache for others.

Furthermore, one can only begin to imagine the short- and long-term ecological damage that the Channel Tunnel will cause in a wide band of the country stretching all the way from the south-east coast to London. New motorways will be built and existing roads will continue to be improved for years to come in order to accommodate massive increases in commercial and tourist traffic using the Tunnel. The Tunnel may bring some advantages, though, if the high-speed rail link is fully used throughout the UK. This possibility will be looked at in 'The develop-and-depart syndrome' on page 129.

In Britain alone the problem is becoming acute. The rate of traffic density growth was highlighted by the Department of Transport (DoT) in its publication *Transport Statistics* (1993). This document shows that between 1982 and 1992 traffic increased by 44 per cent on ordinary roads, and by 100 per cent on motorways. It also predicts that there will be a 100 per cent increase in car ownership by the year 2025, which will naturally lead to more air pollution. Apart from the effects of vehicle emissions on the natural world and the built heritage, scientists are now investigating the links between traffic increase and a growing incidence of asthma and other allergies. A £1 million research programme, backed by the RAC Foundation for Motoring and the Environment and begun in 1993, has already shown that long-term levels of nitrogen dioxide increased in urban areas of the UK by 30 per cent between 1986 and 1991. Overall, motor vehicles cause around 50 per cent of oxides of nitrogen in the air, with cars responsible for half of this. How much more poison can we tolerate?

Visual pollution

Measures to lessen the amount of visual pollution and environmental intrusion caused by main roads and motorways have been suggested in Britain by the DoT. They have produced a *Good Roads Guide* for the use of their own staff and consultants, which suggests ways for roads to blend harmoniously with the environment and reduce noise and air pollution for nearby residents. It outlines practical ways in which lighting, fencing, drainage, signposting and provision for wildlife can all help a new road to fit in with its surroundings. 'Green' roads should:

- follow the contours of the landscape to blend in with the surrounding countryside
- keep off the skyline to minimise impact
- ensure the use of mounding and cutting to screen the road from nearby towns and villages
- involve the planting of trees and shrubs along the roadsides.

Backing for this policy has been given by the Forestry Commission, the Countryside Commission and the Urban Wildlife Trust.

Pollution on the wing

The aeroplane does far more damage to the atmosphere than the motor car and burns up far greater volumes of oxygen. Statistics released in July 1993 by the International Air Transport Association (IATA) show that the total number of passengers carried by IATA airlines on international scheduled routes rose in 1992–93 by 10 per cent to 286 million. In its *Annual Report*, November 1993, IATA predicts that international scheduled service airlines are likely to carry 38 per cent more passengers in 1997 than they did in 1993, estimating annual passenger-number growth at 6.6 per cent. The biggest increase was expected to be on flights to and from eastern and central Europe, as well as south-east and north-east Asia.

These are only the *scheduled* airlines. If world-wide figures for the holiday-charter and domestic-services sectors are added, that figure is more than doubled. Tour operators in Britain alone sold nearly 10 million holidays involving air travel between April and September 1993 – 7 per cent more than in the same period in 1992. Throughout the whole year, tour operators sold more than 14 million air holidays – a rise of 10 per cent on the year before. (Source: *Civil Aviation Authority Report*, January 1994.)

Total current world figures are difficult to obtain, but some idea of the scale of aircraft movement may be gained by looking at statistics for the top two American airlines. United (based in Chicago) claims to be the world's most travelled airline and logged 76.4 *billion* passenger miles in the first nine months of 1993; American (based at Fort Worth) came next with 74.63 billion.

A study by Dr Mark Barret and Adam Markham (*Aircraft Pollution: Environmental Impacts and Future Solutions*, 1991) which was undertaken for the World Wide Fund for Nature (WWF) has revealed that more British people are now travelling further afield to take their holidays. This move towards distant destinations like India, Hong Kong, Malaysia, Honolulu and Australia means more high-altitude flights. Thailand, for example, has enjoyed a tourist boom in the 1990s and now caters for over five million visitors a year. Dr Barret notes that business travel in the UK accounts for only 20 per cent of flights, and that 80 per cent of journeys are to holiday destinations. He therefore recommends improving the leisure environment nearer home to encourage people not to travel so far when taking vacations. Mr Markham, his co-author, who is head of resources consumption and pollution policy at WWF, points out that there is new scientific data to suggest that air transport may be contributing between 5 and 40 per cent to additional global warming:

> The bulk of emissions of nitrogen oxide from aircraft are produced at cruising heights, typically 10–12 kilometres, where they are extremely effective in creating ozone.
> Unfortunately, this is exactly the altitude at which ozone has most impact as a greenhouse gas.

How does air traffic grow?

The amount of air traffic is continually increasing as new destinations for tourism are opened up. What were formerly simple landing fields or clearings in the forest are soon turned into bustling modern airports as the powerful jet aircraft needed for long-haul flights operate around the clock and bring in tourists from all destinations by the million.

Aircraft are growing larger and consequently consume more fuel and oxygen. The McDonnell Douglas 83, for instance, one of the smaller modern planes, is popular with both scheduled and charter airlines. It carries 167 passengers at 560 mph, has a range of 4,630 km (2,500 nautical miles), reaches a maximum altitude of 11,277 m (37,000 feet), and uses 26,495 l (7,800 gallons) of high-grade kerosene on a full-range flight. The Boeing 767–200 wide-bodied jet aircraft is considerably bigger, carrying 282 passengers and costing £50 million to build. It has almost twice the range (4,800 nautical miles) and uses correspondingly more fuel. Boeing created the first jumbo jet, the wide-bodied, four-engined 747, variations of which are still in use around the world. Now plans have been completed for Boeing to combine with British Aerospace and Daimler Benz of Germany to build a new 650-seat super-jumbo jetliner within the next few years.

National airlines are the pathfinders of tourism

The big international tour operators open up a new resort by buying or building hotels and other holiday accommodation. They then make agreements with the national airline of the host country to bring out visitors from various tourism-generating regions. When the volume of passengers is too great for national airlines to handle, the non-scheduled airlines, in which the tour operators have a large investment, bring in more and more customers from all around the globe. So the situation escalates and another quiet place becomes a 'tropical paradise', soon to be a destination occupying three or four pages of the holiday brochures. Within two or three years major airports are built to add to the sum of the world's air and noise pollution.

Advantages of the Channel Tunnel for the Environment

Dr Barret's recommendation about cutting air travel may carry more weight when the high-speed Eurostar train which links Paris to London under the English Channel becomes fully operational. This ¼-mile-long luxury train will carry 800 passengers between the two capitals in three hours; the service aims to compete fiercely with short-haul airline services ('short haul' is defined by airlines as a flight with a journey length of up to 350/400 miles, e.g.

London/Paris/Brussels/Amsterdam/Frankfurt, etc.). The operators of Eurostar say it will be 'like flying under the sea', with speeds reaching 100 mph in Britain, but up to 186 mph on French tracks. The service operates five times daily, and from 1995 will go direct to Edinburgh, Newcastle, Manchester, Birmingham and York. This high-speed service works in conjunction with *Le Shuttle*, Euro-tunnel's daily, 24-hour train service carrying cars and their passengers between the British and the French coasts. If successful, the Tunnel would therefore eventually lead to fewer planes (as well as fewer cars and coaches). It is even estimated that the new services could replace 20 per cent of the air traffic which now serves these short-haul routes. The result would be fewer carbon emissions, less nitrogen oxide and less congestion.

The develop-and-depart syndrome

Independent travellers, who have the leisure time and resources to avoid package travel, are usually the ones who blaze a trail for large-scale development in an area. Tour operators are always on the lookout for little-known, unspoiled spots with a sunny climate, good, clean beaches and the potential for 'exclusive' developments. For a time such a place becomes a luxurious five-star destination, offering a first-class holiday experience. The friendly local people are charming, trusting, honest and only too pleased to meet new-comers from another part of the world. They offer their services in dignified exchange for the surplus cash of the visitors. The governments of these areas are delighted to cooperate in the siting and construction of high-quality, low profile hotels and other visitor facilities. These have little negative impact and the foreign money gives a boost to an economy often founded on agriculture, fishing, or such like. The existing infrastructure (with some additions funded by foreign money and local investment capital and facilitated by the pool of cheap local labour) is capable of absorbing a few hundred extra, temporary residents.

Within a short time, the place becomes fashionable and the four-star operators move in. Some rather less expensive, higher-density holiday accommodation is built, and for a time four- and five-star holidays exist side by side with little diminution of quality.

Large-scale, world-wide advertising begins, demand increases dramatically and three-star enterprises are developed at popular prices. They flourish and expand as mass marketing brings prices down. Food, toiletries, fittings, skilled labour and international operating personnel are brought in from outside. Four-star operators become uneasy in the face of intense price competition, rising local costs and deterioration in the quality of the tourism experience. Five-star operators depart.

Two-star operators start to take an interest in the area. They bring in many more tourists as part of charter tours. The source markets are bombarded with advertising. More hotels and blocks of self-catering accommodation are built – some in unspoilt coastal areas and surrounding countryside. They become overcrowded and understaffed. More hasty and badly planned construction becomes necessary with the result that vegetation and wildlife have to give way to concrete and asphalt. There is no attempt at environmental management, and commercialism is unchecked. Local infrastructure cannot cope with the pressure of numbers, and resources such as natural supplies of fresh water and clean sea water are overused.

As the image of this formerly beautiful and unspoilt area begins to be tarnished, four-star operators who, like all travel companies do not feel that they owe a loyalty to any particular destination, move on to somewhere less congested. Two-star firms begin to offer more cheap tours. The tourist infrastructure and superstructure grow so rapidly that they encroach on or displace old-established local communities and swamp national culture. Pollution, noise, standards of visitor conduct, traffic flow and congestion develop into problems, which become generally known to the holidaytaking public at all levels. Business begins to drop off and prices come down. Only two-star operators still remain, and even they have to unload holidays at bargain-basement prices achieved by making cut-throat deals with locally based interests. Half of the ill-constructed and badly maintained accommodation stands empty. Local staff become redundant.

The natural and the built environment have been spoilt beyond recall. Agriculture and fishing have been badly affected by pollution; traditional skills have been neglected and lost. Once the boom is over it is discovered that most of the billions spent by foreign visitors have melted away. Some of the money has enriched a few private, local entrepreneurs, but most has gone to big multinational enterprises. (It has been estimated that if both airlines and hotels are owned by foreign companies, only 22–5 per cent of the retail price paid by each tourist helps the economy of the host country.) Money has also leaked back out of the economy to pay for the imported luxuries which tourists demand. The resulting situation pleases no one. This is the classic downward spiral that has provoked the critical attitudes considered at the beginning of this chapter. In the past 50 years the diminution-of-quality syndrome has often been repeated around the coasts of the Mediterranean (including North Africa), the shores of the Balearic Islands, the Greek Islands, Malta and the Atlantic coast of Portugal. The same cycle has begun in Madeira and the Canary Islands, as these destinations become most popular with those with modest holiday budgets.

Improvements in travel technology ensure that distances are shrinking, and copycat situations can be observed around the world from the Maldives to Indonesia, from Florida to the Caribbean, from the Gambia to the Seychelles. Some of these places continue to cater for quite expensive long-haul bookings, but mass mobility continues to expand and there have been tourist booms recently in South America, Cuba and Vietnam simply because these destinations are offering cheaper holidays and more cut-price, long-stay breaks than anywhere else. The trend for taking holidays on the other side of the world is growing rapidly among the populations of the northern hemisphere as air fares are progressively reduced. The heat-seeking tourist, it has been said, is more deadly to the environment than the heat-seeking missile!

In practical terms there is little anyone can do to issue bans on travel or prohibit transport development – it is scarcely conceivable that the rapid expansion in travel by aircraft, cruise ships, coaches, trains and private cars could be brought to an end because of ecological considerations. If the technology is there it will be used: it inevitably creates its own demand. It would be undemocratic as well as totally impracticable to deny people the right to take advantage of cheaper holiday prices. We can never put the clock back to the situation outlined in Chapter 2, when overseas holidays were the privilege of a lucky few and the mass of the population of any country simply stayed at home like their parents and grandparents before them. How can these conflicting interests be resolved?

Signs of awareness and conscience

What answers can the tourist industry give to the charges that it is thoughtlessly polluting the planet? Presenting the Tourism for Tomorrow awards in 1992 at the Natural History Museum, London, the celebrated conservationist, Dr David Bellamy, voiced the opinion that tourism might actually help to save the world by opening up people's eyes. He said that there was a growing will to halt the destruction of natural vegetation and landscape as well as the extinction of plants and animals, and added:

> That will is growing thanks to the fact that people can travel and see both the problems and the potential for themselves. Tourism was a two-edged sword hanging over the once-green world. Now one of its blades is being re-shaped into the ploughshare of knowledge which can save the world.

David Bellamy

It is worth considering this optimistic statement, and trying to find some evidence of tourism initiatives that help to create a more responsible and sustainable industry. The following are just a few examples from the voluntary, commercial and state sectors.

The voluntary sector

A growing number of conservation holidays are on offer to people with a conscience about the environment who want to volunteer to study the Earth's problems and actually do something about them. Work ranges from spending a weekend helping to restore wildlife habitats and pond-clearing in Sussex or on an organic farm in Wales to surveying a coral reef, tracking dolphins in the Bahamas or studying orang-utans in Borneo.

The National Trust relies increasingly on volunteers and runs working holidays called Acorn Projects and Oak Camps. The British Trust for Conservation Volunteers organises similar breaks for dry-stone walling, coppicing woodland, laying hedges and clearing disused canals. The Royal Society for the Protection of Birds offers the chance to spend a holiday acting as a volunteer warden at any one of their 30 reserves throughout Britain, observing bird life and doing a variety of conservation work.

On a world-wide scale this type of work can be undertaken by joining a project run by Earthwatch, a worthwhile institution founded over 20 years ago in America that provides funding and volunteers for scientific research projects around the globe. Its founders describe it as:

> A once-in-a-lifetime opportunity to serve your world in the company of dedicated experts; your chance to give something back.

Teams are sent out to conduct rainforest research in the Upper Amazon, explore the Barrier Reef, investigate dolphin intelligence in Hawaii or survey the rhino population of Zimbabwe, to give but a few examples of their work.

The commercial sector

Not every venture can be voluntary, but some tour operators, although they operate on a profit-making basis, do take conservation very seriously and make contributions to 'green' charities. Discover The World is one such commercial company that works with internationally respected organisations like the World Wide Fund for Nature, the Whale and Dolphin Conservation Society (WDCS) and the Royal Society for Nature Conservation. The great benefit which such operators give us is the ability to observe wildlife and remote places for ourselves so that we can learn to respect and care for the Earth and its inhabitants.

Transocean Cruise Lines has a specially built, environmentally friendly vessel (the *Columbus Caravelle*), which carries 250 passengers who want to gain experience of lands, peoples, cultures and wildlife far off the usual beaten track of tourism. The ship has a lecture room where experts in archaeology, marine biology and wildlife supply information about the sights to be seen. Most importantly, the company has a firm commitment to preserve and not disturb the natural habitats and environments of the places it visits.

Tours like these confirm Dr Bellamy's theory perfectly. Even more convincingly, while whale hunters are still taking out their boats, they are now leaving their harpoons at home and filling their craft with cargoes of tourists taking organised whale-watching trips. The most encouraging fact is that this type of holiday is growing most rapidly in Japan – a country which kills whales and dolphins for so-called 'scientific' purposes and continues to consume the meat of these animals as a delicacy. The WDCS believes that over the next 15 years the tourist trade could earn the Japanese whaling community nine times the revenue it would make from slaughtering its diminishing stocks of endangered whales. This incentive should be a much more effective way of protecting these creatures than passing laws and issuing bans on hunting.

The state sector

The Galapagos archipelago is a group of small volcanic islands in the South Pacific, 600 miles west of Ecuador. There are 13 main islands, and hundreds of small, uninhabited islets. The islands became well known as a result of the writings of Charles Darwin who visited them in 1835 during the expeditionary voyage of the *Beagle*. The wildlife he saw there confirmed the theories he was developing about natural selection that later appeared in his revolutionary book, *On the Origin of Species*. Darwin saw the Galapagos Islands as a 'living laboratory' of reptiles and birds that had evolved in isolation in this remote spot. Other scientists followed in his footsteps, and inevitably behind them came the curious and the sightseers. Colonists have also come to settle and work on these bleak and inhospitable islands. Recently, uncontrolled immigration has been permitted so that colonists arriving from the US, Europe and Ecuador have in the last 20 years trebled the population to 12,000. There is no doubt that, but for the profitable tourist trade, they would overfish and hunt to extinction the giant tortoises, iguanas, boobies, cormorants and albatrosses. The inhabitants would also destroy, in the course of using modern farming methods, the rare plants that survive there.

Ecuador is a poor country with a fragile economy and the government in Quito was quick to see the importance of the islands' tourist industry as a major source of foreign currency. A landing tax of US $40 per person, plus other taxes, brings in more than $50 million a year to the Ecuadorean Treasury. Thirty years ago there were fewer than 20 visitors a week, but now, in spite of this hefty entrance levy, numbers have had to be officially limited to 25,000 annually. It is believed, though, that thousands more tourists sneak in from cruise boats, and that the true number might be as high as 80,000 a year. Realising, fortunately, that unrestricted tourism would cause colossal damage to the delicate ecosystem through erosion and pollution, Ecuador has firmly resisted appeals for massive hotel developments on the archipelago. Clearly, if the wildlife were to be destroyed, no tourists would visit, and so the Ecuadorean government designated the Galapagos one of its national parks; it is also a World Heritage Site.

The government now works with the scientists at the Charles Darwin Foundation, the United Nations Educational, Scientific and Cultural Organisation (UNESCO) and the International Union for the Conservation of Nature (IUCN) to monitor the effects of tourism and carry out breeding programmes. In theory, visitors are only allowed on shore at 45 carefully selected sites and must be in groups of 10 or fewer. They must be accompanied by a licensed guide, keep to the marked paths, never touch the wildlife and leave by sunset. All ships must be licensed and visitors are encouraged to stay on the cruisers and mini-liners which bring them. The number of licences is restricted and crews are given training to stop them indulging in damaging habits like throwing rubbish overboard. It is heartening to see the longer-term ecological view being taken by the authorities, and the more common over-exploiting commercial attitude rejected.

Sadly, however, even on these few highly-protected square miles, no government can legislate completely against the weakness and foolishness of *Homo sapiens*. Settlers have brought with them pigs, goats, horses, cattle, cats, and dogs. Over the course of time some of these have run wild and, along with the rats and insects which have come off ships for over a century, have upset the delicate environmental balance that had developed over millions of years.

There have been two disastrous fires on Isabela which, at 50 miles long by 37 miles wide, is the archipelago's largest island. The first, in 1985, was started by farmers burning off brush and lasted for 75 days. Almost 100,000 acres of the national park were destroyed, and quite a few of the giant tortoises (*Galápagos* in Spanish means tortoise) died in the heat. The second blaze was started on 11 April 1994 by the camp fires of some of the poachers who prey upon the islands' rare and endangered species. On this occasion, 16,000 acres were burned in the conflagration which

A giant tortoise of the Galapagos Islands

135

raged for 15 days. It is thought possible that the rail (a flightless bird) and many of Isabela's 1,000 insect species have been lost. Only the efforts of an international team which included local volunteers, units of the Ecuadorean Army and Civil Defence Force, Canadian firefighters, and US forest ecologists stopped the fire just short of the Sierra Negra volcano which is the nesting area of the giant tortoises. How sad it would have been if these unique creatures – which can weigh as much as 500 pounds and live so long that Darwin himself may have observed some of the very same animals – had been completely wiped out as a result of human greed and callousness.

Preserving paradise

A very sensible view has been taken by the Indian government which has turned the Lakshadweep Islands into a nature reserve that will have its outstanding natural beauty protected. There are 36 islands lying in the Arabian Sea, 290 miles off the tip of India. Visitors can visit other islands but have only recently been allowed to stay on one, Bangaram. The only accommodation is a collection of simple huts near the beach. There are no telephones, faxes, television sets or newspapers. There is absolutely no litter: conservation and the environment are taken very seriously and all non-degradable rubbish has to be shipped back to the mainland for disposal. The aim is to protect this uncommercialised paradise from over-development and preserve it for future generations to enjoy.

Advertising

As noted earlier advertising is necessary to the tourism industry; it is all the more welcome, however, if it is responsible and makes a sensible appeal to the better part of our nature. Invitations such as:

> Lose yourself in our private paradise. Discover the meaning of luxury. Sample pure indulgence. Experience nothing but pleasure. Everything is laid on for you.

or:

> Wild, quirky, out-of-the-way islands attract wild, quirky, out-of-the-way people. And if ever there was a home for sun-bleached eccentrics, it is the often forgotten corner of the Caribbean called the Turks and Caicos Islands.

do seem to invite an uncaring response and carry overtones of exploitation.

Much more encouraging is the advertising of the South African government, who have worked with private enterprise to develop the Conservation Corporation, a body totally committed to protecting the environment and the life that inhabits it. Their advert states:

> The Conservation Corporation is committed to wildlife conservation in Africa. Through reserves such as Londolozi, Phinda and Nagala, we aim not only to provide guests with an exceptional wildlife experience, but also to promote ecological sustainability. To create a partnership with local communities. And to rebuild the land.
>
> Experience Landrover and walking safaris with knowledgeable guides. Explore diverse ecosystems. And discover some of the best game viewing in South Africa.

This responsible approach makes a welcome contrast to the sort of advertising that only 40 years ago encouraged so-called 'sportsmen' to take their toll of wildlife while collecting trophies of animal heads and skins.

Changing attitudes

Education about all aspects of conservation has improved enormously in recent years. Through work in schools and colleges, television and radio programmes, articles in the press and the efforts of voluntary bodies, enlightened attitudes are spreading throughout the world. It has begun to look as though there might be hope for the Earth. Perhaps most encouraging of all is that children are leading the trend to be critical of bodies that do not adopt a sympathetic attitude on environmental and consumer issues. Young people who are well informed, sensitive and alert make very good guardians of the environment, and companies who show a disregard for green issues will lose business now and in the future. An example of this new awareness can be seen in the following 'Holiday Code' which is printed in all the brochures of Thomson, the largest UK tour operator:

> We'd appreciate it if you would spare a few minutes to consider how you can help care for the local environment when you're abroad.
>
> If everyone does a little, we can all achieve considerable reductions in the pressures that tourism brings to holiday resort areas.
>
> **• Do . . . save water**
>
> Water is a precious resource especially in all hot climates. So, if you can, take short showers and make sure you turn off all taps. Report water leaks immediately.

- **Do . . . guard against fire**

In hot, dry countries a carelessly discarded cigarette or a picnic fire could easily start a woodland blaze.

- **Do . . . respect the peace and quiet of others**

We all enjoy some peace and quiet on holiday – loud noise can be annoying, so please think of your fellow guests.

- **Do . . . protect local wildlife**

Many animals are protected by law. Please don't buy exotic souvenirs made of turtle shell, ivory, reptile skins, furs, feathers or coral.

- **Don't . . . litter**

Discarded litter is an eyesore, so even if you see others litter, make sure you take yours away for proper disposal.

- **Don't . . . waste energy**

Always switch off lights and electrical or gas appliances when not in use.

- **Don't . . . ignore the Country Code:**
  – Fasten all gates
  – Keep to paths when crossing farmland
  – Avoid damaging fences, hedges and walls
  – Respect the life of the countryside

- **Don't . . . collect coral, shells, reef animals or other underwater 'treasures'**

Thomson also has an environment department run by its own staff; at the end of the 'Holiday Code' it states:

The paper used in the production of this brochure has been carefully selected with due consideration for the environment. It is made from trees grown as a commercial, renewable resource: for every tree felled at least two are planted to replace it.

Carriers, too, have their commitment to the environment, and British Airways offers the following suggestions to travellers:

- Please resist the temptation to take 'souvenirs' from historical sites and national parks.
- If you go snorkelling or diving please remember that coral is a sensitive living organism.
- Travel light; conserve energy.
- **Leave only footprints and take only photographs.**
- Seek out the more 'environmental' tourist attractions and activities.

The support or voluntary sector is naturally very active in trying to educate travellers. The Ark Foundation has launched a 'Green Travel Bug Campaign' and offers *Go For It*, a free colour brochure with practical hints for travellers on how to minimise their impact on holiday destinations. In addition to making all the points listed above, this publication advises:

- Be considerate – remember your holiday resort is someone else's home.
- Be kind to wildlife – loud music, bonfires, litter and off-road driving can disturb or destroy animals, birds and plants.
- Always seek permission before taking photographs of people, and respect their privacy.
- Support traditional local skills by buying crafts made in the area.
- Get to know the country and the people better by walking or cycling and eating at local restaurants.

Many examples of practical ways of reducing the pollution caused by tourism could be given, but there is only space to look at two initiatives that have proved successful in Britain. Much has been written about the damage being caused to the Norfolk Broads by the high volume of boating traffic in the holiday season. In response to criticism of boats being 'the great destroyers' of the Broads, the Phoenix Fleet, which has been established for 30 years, now uses electric day-boats. They ask visitors to:

See and hear the beauty and wildlife of the Norfolk Broads from a quiet, pollution-free Electric Day Boat. Almost silent electric motors power the boats for up to ten hours. Sleek and beautifully designed hulls create little wash, causing the least disturbance to other river users and wildlife.

The second example of good practice comes appropriately from the activities of the National Trust, the world's largest conservation organisation. The NT has an annual power bill of £2.5 million for its 200 properties in England and Wales, and has developed an environmental policy to cut its electricity and gas costs by 10 per cent. Work undertaken so far in harnessing green energy includes:

- solar-powered pumps to flush the lavatories at the Cragside estate in Northumberland, where Cragside House is already lit by electricity from a wind turbine
- the restoration of water wheels and windmills on sites of industrial archaeology for use as energy sources; Europe's biggest waterwheel at the Aberdulais Falls in West Glamorgan has been restored to drive a 200-kilowatt turbine and supply power to the historic industrial site

- a hydro-electric plant on the Malham Tarn estate
- the use of renewable energy, including the burning of straw, coppiced timber and other products from the NT's many estates.

Heritage interpretation

If travellers are to have meaningful experiences on holiday it is preferable that the authentic qualities of the built environment should be preserved as far as possible, and that where there are replicas, substitutes and re-creations they should be identified as such. This raises further questions about heritage presentation:

- What artefacts should be preserved and displayed to make a worthwhile yet attractive exhibition?
- What aspects of the past are to be highlighted to become part of the shared image for future cultural identity?
- Is the presentation (e.g. lifelike animatronic models; sound and light effects; diorama displays; riding in an automatic guided vehicle, etc.) more important than the content?

If people come to gaze in awe at the legacy of history, the tourism industry should at least be honest about what it offers them. Any display that attempts to be educational as well as entertaining should have a basis of reality, and though judicious restoration will sometimes be necessary, there must be a substantial basis of genuine period elements and sound scholarship. History can be revived or re-interpreted but it can never be re-invented. Each ancient place has its own unique spirit and atmosphere. Reproduction castles made of re-inforced concrete, plaster or fibreglass are no substitute for the high, solid towers and thick stone walls of the real thing. They can never inspire the mixture of awe and horror that we feel when we look at the actual edifices of a distant brutal age that still carry an aura of violence and hardship.

The debt to Disney

As noted earlier, the world is becoming full of themed attractions that have given the tourist industry a boost and provided entertainment for young and old alike. Most of these have taken some kind of inspiration from the late Walt Disney, who might be said to have invented the theme park. As far back as 1955 he had the idea of transferring film illusions into a multi-media, walk- or ride-around fantasy environment that lets the visitor travel from the dawn of time into projections of the future. Unlike previous amusement parks, in his Disneyland creation in California everything was planned. From the outset it was safe, clean, arguably educational and faithful to its theme. In 1972 Disney World opened at Orlando in Florida: everybody who has had anything to do with tourism and travel knows what a financial and social success this state-of-the-art, computer-controlled, electronic wonderland has proved to be.

Even more encouraging as far as the environment is concerned is the fact that the Walt Disney company has agreed to help develop 8,500 acres of Florida swampland near Poinciana as a wilderness preserve. Disney will work with the Nature Conservancy Environmental Group to restore the land to its natural state and re-establish wildlife.

As noted already, EuroDisney did not appear as immediately successful as its American equivalents, although there is no doubting its immense touristic impact. What we must ask ourselves, though, is whether we really want this 'imagineering' (the professional dreaming up and executing of three-dimensional fantasies) to be brought to bear on our European heritage. Would the French really welcome a suitably child-orientated 'French Revolution Experience'? In 1993 British, French and US officials agreed to set up a museum devoted to their military presence in Berlin, once on the Cold War's front line. A museum is acceptable and even valuable, but would the German people be any more enthusiastic about 'The Berlin Cold War Spy Theme Park' than we would be about having a 'Merrie England World' built on the outskirts of London? Such places can now easily be created by using multimedia tricks from the stage, cinema, video studio, animatronic workshop and so on. However, it is possible to have too much of a good thing, and leisure consultants are already using the word 'Disneyfication' to refer to the transformation of historic places and customs into trivial entertainment for tourists. Can such 'attractions' really be regarded as cultural? Can they genuinely provide information and education?

Worthwhile developments in the UK

In Britain the decay of industry has sometimes proved to be the saviour of the environment. As the works, foundries, factories and chemical plants disappear, fish return to the rivers, ugly industrial sites are cleared to be replaced by greenery, and the health of local populations is improved. Some relics of the Industrial Revolution are preserved as interpretive centres which bring to life again the trades and everyday activities of those who once lived and worked there. Buildings which are of historical importance are restored and, when not surrounded by the crush of modern traffic, can be viewed as they were one or two centuries ago. A renovated canal, too, can be a corridor for commerce as well as a leisure amenity, a tourist attraction, an environmental advantage and a study centre for industrial archaeology. More and more such venues are appearing on the tourist map every year, and there are now more than enough to justify the writing of a guide book on the subject. The Albert Dock in Liverpool, the Wigan Pier Centre and the Ironbridge Gorge Museum are only three examples taken at random from many.

In 1993 the ETB promoted 'Industrial Heritage Year' through its campaign 'Experience the Making of Britain'. This concentrated on helping visitors to discover how 200 years of innovation and enterprise changed our society and influenced the whole world.

Public awareness

An EU survey (*European Business and the Environment*, 1992) showed a significant increase in public awareness about environmental problems.

- 85 per cent of Europeans believed that environmental protection was 'an immediate and vital problem'
- 90 per cent were worried about the increasing number of cars and lorries on the road
- 94 per cent said they avoided dropping litter
- 84 per cent said they tried to save energy
- 83 per cent were sorting household waste for recycling
- 81 per cent were saving water
- 73 per cent were making less noise
- 48 per cent said they would be prepared to go on a type of holiday that was less harmful to the environment
- 30 per cent said they were already members of an association for environmental protection, or were ready to join such an organisation.

Governments and tourist boards all around the world are 'thinking green' and studies are being commissioned to set up eco-tourism projects. There are already moves afoot in EU countries to make environmental impact assessments compulsory before further forms of tourist development can take place. The consumer-led movement towards sustainable tourism shows clearly that tour operators without an environmental conscience will see profits drop dramatically. No company can flourish now without a commitment to value people and care for their environment. We must all help to develop a credible scenario for the Earth's future – 'Be kind to the Earth; be kind to people', would be a good motto to adopt.

Assignment: Arranging a package for sustainable tourism

You may find some of the information in Case Study 1 helpful when completing this assignment.

1 Using road maps and Ordnance Survey maps for North Wales, find the exact position of the Centre for Alternative Technology (CAT), Machynlleth, Powys SY20 9AZ. Describe the position of CAT briefly, and illustrate the site's relationship to the town of Machynlleth by means of a simple sketch map. Give road numbers and show landmarks such as rivers and railway lines.

2 Write a letter to CAT asking for a guidebook and a list of the CAT's other publications (the cost of the book is £1.50). Draw an outline map of Britain and within that indicate the position of Machynlleth in relation to the Snowdonia National Park and the Welsh coast.

3 Write about 250 words on what CAT is trying to do.

4 List the working exhibits by which CAT shows how its beliefs can be put into practice.

5 Which of the exhibits do you find the most interesting?

6 Describe the ways in which CAT tries to attract family groups. What provision is made for the elderly and the disabled?

7 How does CAT try to put its educational aims into practice?

8 What means of raising income, apart from point-of-entry charges, does CAT have?

9 Working in groups, plan a short-break package (over a weekend, or three or five days) that features a visit to CAT. You should use maps and information from tourist information centres (TICs) to arrange an itinerary which will offer parties of visitors a chance to spend time at CAT as well as offering experience of other attractions.

- You might consider combining learning about Wales with encouraging environmental awareness and including venues for fun and relaxation. Coastal resorts, mountain trails, heritage properties and gardens, the 'green' power station within a mountain – Dinorwig, a Site of Special Scientific Interest (SSSI), museums, aquaria, indoor 'tropical' water sports centres, various industrial heritage sites and places of special interest to children are all tourist attractions within easy reach of Machynlleth.
- You will have to choose somewhere to stay, somewhere to eat and you will have to consider prices while trying to

arrange the best options. There is a wide range of accommodation in the area including campsites, self-catering cabins,
farms, guest houses and hotels of various grades.

- In addition, you will have to arrange transport. How this is
done will depend on whether you intend to plan for clients
to make their own way to the base in Wales from which you
intend to operate, or to collect them from various points *en
route*. The size of your party and the cost per head will also
influence your choice of transport.

10 Arrange a presentation to sell your group's short break to
an audience. In this you will have to outline an advertising
and promotional campaign for your package. You will also
have to consider arrangements for the health and safety of customers and other legal obligations imposed by UK and EU
regulations.

Case Study 1
The village of the future

The Centre for Alternative Technology (CAT) near Machynlleth, Powys, Mid-Wales was established in 1974 as a 'green', self-contained community designed to promote technologies that sustain rather than damage the environment. It was intended that the community should demonstrate to other people the options for them to achieve positive change in their own lives through:

- *inspiring* – instilling the desire to change by practical example
- *informing* – feeding the desire to change by providing the most appropriate information
- *enabling* – providing effective and continuing support to put the change into practice.

After 20 years of research and practical work CAT's reputation and influence throughout the world has grown steadily. It is now the largest 'green' visitor attraction in Europe and an educational centre that draws visitors from all over the world. It has become a tourist destination in its own right; **in 1992 95,000 people visited CAT**.

Part of this success comes from its beautiful and unspoiled location in the Welsh hills close to the mountain splendour of Snowdonia and within easy reach of a picturesque stretch of coast. A conscious effort has been made to create a venue that will appeal to a wide range of visitors. There is a whole host of interesting educational displays and demonstrations set in the 7-acre site and a day can easily be spent browsing around the exhibits, just as in any conventional theme park. An alpine railway takes visitors from the car park to the top of the steep cliff-face above which the Centre is situated. Before the railway was constructed (in 1992–93) access was by a steep 300-yard path that was particularly difficult for the elderly, the disabled and families with young children. The railway, with its Swiss-style upper and lower stations, is itself an

The alpine railway at the Centre for Alternative Technology in Powys

attraction and is operated on the water-balancing principle used by Victorian engineers for seaside cliff railways. The power comes from an attractive new feeder lake that now provides an ornamental feature and a focus for wildlife. The hydraulics are controlled by a computerised weighing system which, in keeping with the philosophy of the site, ensures a safe, energy-efficient method of transportation. The cliff railway received an award from the BTA British Guild of Travel Writers and a British Airways Tourism for Tomorrow award in 1993.

There is an adventure playground for older children, a toddlers' play area, an unusual maze and a children's recycling area. Also popular with children is the animal enclosure, where there are families of chickens, ducks, goats and pigs that have been raised and kept in accordance with humane and environmentally friendly guidelines.

Catering facilities are provided by a wholefood restaurant that maintains very high food and beverage (F & B) standards, and is Egon Ronay recommended. Across from the restaurant stands the store which is reputed to house one of Britain's best-stocked environmental bookshops as well as a wide range of eco-friendly goods and gifts.

Since 1979 CAT has been running residential courses for the general public. Accommodation is provided in the cabins facility which is under the guidance of a resident tutor-warden. Such courses offer a more leisurely, in-depth look at alternative technologies, ranging from weekend breaks to week-long study programmes, and are concerned with the subjects and skills for which CAT has become famous – wind power, water power, solar collectors and organic growing. The most popular course is Self Build (DIY). The Centre teaches the Segal method, which was developed particularly for those self builders with no or minimal building knowledge. **In 1992, 300 people attended CAT's residential and business courses**.

School parties can be accommodated and are taught educational courses that attract a wide spectrum of interested people, from primary school children to lecturers and international experts on ecological subjects. CAT has its own education officers, who can arrange for courses to be taught in Welsh or French if required. Tutors are also available to make advisory visits and give outside lectures and seminars for schools, colleges, universities and the general public. **In 1992 15,000 students visited the Centre. 3,000 of these stayed for residential courses; the remainder stayed for day visits**.

An information and research service is available by telephone or post and is also open to personal callers. CAT maintains comprehensive data banks and publishes scores of books and pamphlets (printed on environmentally friendly card and recycled paper) that cover a wide range of environmental issues. The staff deal with hundreds of enquiries every week from individuals, private companies, environmental organisations and government departments. **CAT receives approximately 20,000 enquiries each year. Of these 60 per cent are telephone enquiries; the remainder are postal**.

The Centre is currently engaged in completing and equipping its Passive Solar Study Centre in conjunction with the University of North London's Low Energy Architectural Research Unit (LEARN). This new building will contain a computerised information office, workshop, lecture theatre and 10 study bedrooms. The cost on completion will be over £1 million. However, the innovative method of passive solar construction was considered so exceptional that the EU provided a grant of £240,000 under its Thermie programme for energy-efficient technologies. It is hoped that the remainder of the money will be raised from trusts and foundations, business sponsorship and donations from CAT's world-wide membership, supporters and visitors.

The displays and demonstrations, that are open to the public, also have a practical application in that they sustain a residential community. There are more than 30 permanent staff members, who include among their number environmentalists, engineers, architects, builders, teachers, horticulturalists, biologists and others. The Centre is not connected to a mains electricity supply, and the power needed to run the site comes from renewable (wind, water and solar) sources. There is as much concentration on energy-saving as on energy production, and the Centre's engineers say: 'If necessary we can keep the entire site running on the power equivalent of a large electric kettle.' The organic garden produces food uncontaminated by pesticides, hormones or additives and all waste products are recycled.

The principles of alternative technology state that human needs should be provided for by methods that are:

- *sustainable* – that do not exhaust the resources from which they spring; that can be continued indefinitely and leave the world a better place
- *economical* – that use resources frugally, carefully and efficiently
- *equitable* – that do not operate at the expense of others; that would be sustainable even if universally adopted
- *natural* – that work in harmony with the natural forces of the Earth, physical and biological
- *interdependent* – that appreciate the links between issues such as health, work, consumption and the environment; a true solution to a problem in one area is found only by looking at the effects of any action on them all.

If these principles were followed by tourism suppliers, they would be seen to answer many of the criticisms of the industry that were noted in Chapter 5. Is it possible to apply these ideas to package tourism?

Case Study 2
Biarritz, health and tourism

A beautiful region of the Basque Country has capitalised on its natural advantages and developed a thriving tourist industry without overexploitation of places or people. The downward spiral of 'develop and depart' that was noted in Chapter 5 has been avoided by careful planning, exercising quality control and working in conjunction with the inhabitants to safeguard the natural and built environments.

It was decided that the area's clean beaches and coastal waters along with its climatic and scenic resources should be utilised to promote modern health and beauty treatments, golf, tennis, yachting, water sports, riding, mountaineering and hill walking. These projects in the health and fitness industries were underpinned by emphasising the rich and varied folklore of the Basque people and taking steps to preserve their strong cultural identity. Visitors are offered the best of regional and international food and drink, and there is a wide choice from special health diets to classic gastronomic menus. In addition, there is plentiful provision of attractions for those who are interested in the fine arts. As well as permanent collections in museums and art galleries there are seasonal festivals of painting and sculpture, poetry, music and theatre; and museums which specialise in archaeology, decorative arts and history. The Oceanographic Museum has galleries and displays of fishing and climate, whale hunting in former days, ocean recreation, cliffs and erosion. There are 24 illuminated aquaria in this marine museum, and several seapool reserves which attract serious students as well as family groups.

Location

The Basque Country is a compact area straddling the Western Pyrenees on the Atlantic seaboard. There are seven Basque provinces, four in Spain (Navarra, Guipuzcoa, Biscaye and Alava) and three in France (Labourd, Basse Navarre and Soule).

Language

In spite of linguistic and cultural influences from both France and Spain the Basque language, Euskara, has held its ground since Roman times when it was spoken all along the Pyrenean chain. Together with French and Spanish, it is still spoken in a good third of the seven historical Basque provinces.

History

The Basques have a maritime history. They were the first whalers in Europe, and the fact that so many of the coats-of-arms of coastal towns from Biarritz to Bilbao show whaling scenes attests to the importance of the activity since the Middle Ages. Basques were also predominant amongst the early traders and explorers; the shipyards of Bilbao supplied the vessels for the Spanish conquistadors, and Basque sailors, missionaries and merchants were at the forefront in colonising the 'New World'.

The beach at Biarritz

The resort of Biarritz

Biarritz (in the Labourd province) was originally a small Basque whaling station that was transformed into an internationally renowned seaside resort. The fashionable era started at the end of the eighteenth century as the benefits of sea-bathing became appreciated. When the emperor of France, Napoleon III, married the Spanish countess, Eugenie, in 1853, the great days of Biarritz really began. Eugenie knew the town very well, and Napoleon built the Villa Eugenie for her, which became the imperial holiday home of the couple. Royalty, the aristocracy and the rich were drawn to this elegant town throughout the nineteenth century: Queen Victoria, the Prince of Wales, the King of Spain, the Shah of Persia, Grand Duke Nicholas of Russia and a wide circle of European nobles flocked to this, the most fashionable resort in Europe.

The dark years of the 1930s

During the early decades of the twentieth century competition from the Côte d'Azur on the Mediterranean coast of France lured away the rich and famous to newer resorts such as Nice, Cannes and St Tropez. In the 1930s the Wall Street crash and the Spanish Civil War were followed by the Second World War, and the fortunes of Biarritz declined.

The fading image of the French Riviera

The image of the French Riviera has, however, in turn become tarnished since the glory days of the 1950s and '60s when film stars, writers, models, society photographers and great numbers of the well-to-do made it the playground of the fashionable set. There are now complaints that the area is overrun by drug addicts, criminals, unscrupulous commercial operators and penniless drifters. It is also overcrowded by package tourists from all over Europe: this type of trade is now being welcomed at bargain-basement prices. Since the celebrities have departed, the beaches are becoming dirty, standards of public behaviour are falling and the infrastructure is struggling to cope with too many visitors.

Health, beauty and sport in Biarritz

Biarritz has profited by this changed situation, and, building upon its reputation as an exclusive and healthy resort, has succeeded in attracting the top end of the tourist trade. Travel for purposes of health and fitness is one of the acceptable faces of tourism, and Biarritz has established itself as the European centre of excellence. The waters of the Atlantic are cleaner than those of the overcrowded, polluted Mediterranean, so sea-water health treatment is a more attractive proposition along the Basque coast. Modern *thalasso* (sea-water therapy) centres have been constructed and are run in accordance with the latest scientific principles. Teams of qualified physio- and water therapists are employed and give treatment under constant medical surveillance. Such centres have to be approved by the Regional Commission for Health and Care Establishments in Aquitaine. Some of the large hotels have their own in-house health centres. The Miramar houses the famous Louison Bobet Institution, and the Atlanthal has a sea-water therapy centre covering 1,300 square metres. Patients are often referred by international physicians to the *thalassotherapie* centres of Biarritz, where treatment can be given for rheumatic and arthritic pain, traumatology, spinal disorders, metabolic problems, circulatory problems, obesity, stress-related problems, muscular pain and other complaints.

Many people come to enjoy simple fitness or cosmetic-improvement programmes, rather than to undergo intensive cures. There are extensive facilities for health, sport and beauty care staffed by trained beauticians, dieticians, athletics advisers and sport coaches. Sports provision is much more comprehensive than in most other European resorts. Golf has been established in Biarritz for more than 100 years and it has the second oldest golf course in France, so naturally courses of the highest standard abound throughout the area. Biarritz can also boast 30 years of surfing on its powerfully curling Atlantic waves, and plays host to the world surfing championships. Tennis is firmly established in the area and there are hundreds of first-class courts. A more unusual attraction for tourists is that they can watch, and even participate in, the ancient Basque game of *pelota*.

Mixing business and pleasure

Biarritz has modern facilities to welcome conferences, congresses and conventions, and many prestigious international corporations and learned associations choose the town for their annual business/professional get-togethers. There are conference centres at the Palais de Festivals, seating 230, and at the Convention Center Bellvue, with 600 seats. Both these venues are equipped with the latest communications technology, including simultaneous translation equipment. In addition, every hotel of any size has its *salle de seminaires* or *salle de réunions*, that has audio-visual equipment, a video-transmission network and direct telephone lines to all parts of the world.

There are many attractions to occupy the leisure hours of business people and other visitors in this lively town. Casinos, racecourses, superb shops, night clubs, fine restaurants, firework displays and so on ensure a festive atmosphere, and the Anglet

Municipal Tourism office (1, Avenue de la Chambre D'Amour, 64600 Anglet) emphasises that Biarritz typifies the art of good living as well as the quest for physical fitness. A good proportion of the summer visitors are French nationals who stay with their children for a month or even for the whole of the Continental summer holidays.

Flexible holiday accommodation

Longer stays with families call for more flexible and less expensive alternatives to conventional hotels. There are plenty of self-catering holiday apartments and good permanent camping sites in the Labourd. In addition, the area has many excellent examples of the *hôtel-résidence* or *aparthôtel*. The latter are flexible arrangements of holiday accommodation designed for single persons, couples or families. These apartments have *en suite* bathrooms, kitchen and laundry facilities, television and direct telephone lines. Unlike ordinary holiday apartment blocks, though, there are on-site swimming pools, sun terraces, children's play areas, public rooms, bars, restaurants, sports and fitness facilities and occasional entertainment.

Longer-stay visitors can benefit a resort in several ways. They will feel a greater affinity for a place and form more of a community than short-stay visitors on organised tours. They are also very good for repeat business. This in turn encourages investment in the resort, and means that less has to be spent on advertising and promotion.

Advertising and image

Advertising can regulate the public's perception of a destination, and then maintain a consistent policy to preselect the market it wishes to serve. The Comité de Tourisme et des Fêtes in Biarritz came to the conclusion that it did not make sense to attract 500 short-stay, tight-budget tourists if they only spent the same amount as 50 longer-stay visitors with a higher disposable income. Big tour operators dealing in large numbers of short-stay, rapid-turnover customers at rock-bottom prices would overload the infrastructure and completely change the image of resorts in the Labourd. It would then be the travel companies who dictated the nature of the destinations by advertising and promotion, and who would eventually impose monopolistic control. For this reason you will not find Biarritz advertised alongside Palma, Torremolinos, Rimini, Kos, Lanzarote, Faro, Orlando or any other mass tourism destination.

Why balance and harmony are maintained in Biarritz

Apart from the points made above, and the fact that some smaller travel companies do offer inclusive tours in the Labourd, there are few factors to encourage the larger package-tour operators to target Biarritz. There is no big international airport in the region: the aerodrome at Biarritz-Parme is a small civil establishment that is unsuitable for the large, high-capacity jet aircraft used by charter companies to keep fares down. The nearest airports suitable for such traffic are Toulouse and Bordeaux, and their considerable distance from Biarritz means that transfers would be impractically expensive. There is a bustling railway station at Biarritz, and there are sleeping-trains from Paris, Calais, Lyons and other major French cities and ports. The cost of this type of rail travel is, however, comparatively high and would mean very expensive package travel with low profit margins.

The Labourd is a prosperous region, and unlike emerging countries or the more barren islands and seaboards of the Mediterranean, has a high per capita income. This means that the cost of living is moderately high, and the food and accommodation bargains that attract large-scale operators are rare. This, together with regional planning policy, discourages speculative building.

Most visitors enter the region by car, using the *autoroutes* A63 from Bordeaux or A64 from Toulouse. Some drivers continue along the Spanish motorway A-8 into northern Spain, but most identify the Labourd as an end destination. Traffic also travels the other way along the A-8 *from* Spain. Brittany Ferries, a major UK company operating from Plymouth and Portsmouth, has services to Santander on the Spanish coast (just over 200 miles from Biarritz). Furthermore, in 1993 P & O European ferries started a UK service from Portsmouth to Bilbao, a Spanish port about 180 miles from Biarritz. Their new ship *The Pride of Bilbao* is, at 37,000 tons, the largest ferry ever to operate from the UK. It carries 2,500 passengers and 600 cars on the 30-hour trip. Whether these two services will have a big impact on Biarritz and the Labourd remains to be seen, but it is thought likely that most car drivers will head into northern Spain, which is a spacious region with an excellent Atlantic coast, spectacular scenery and comparatively low prices for food and accommodation.

Index